Preface

Welcome to "Operating System Interview Questions & Answers" This book is designed to be your comprehensive guide to navigating the intricate world of operating systems and acing your interviews in this crucial domain of computer science and IT.

This book is structured to provide a thorough exploration of operating system concepts and to help you prepare for interviews effectively. Inside, you'll find a vast collection of interview questions covering various aspects of operating systems, from the fundamentals to advanced topics. These questions are meticulously crafted to challenge your knowledge and critical thinking, helping you sharpen your problem-solving skills.

Operating systems are complex and multifaceted, and mastering them can be a challenging endeavour. Whether you are a recent graduate preparing for your first job interview or a seasoned professional aiming to stay current in this rapidly evolving field, this book is your comprehensive guide to acing operating system-related interviews.

Interviews for roles in operating systems, system administration, or software development often delve into intricate technical details, problem-solving scenarios, and critical thinking challenges. Our goal with this book is to equip you with the knowledge, skills, and confidence to excel in these interviews. Remember that success in operating systems and interviews is not just about memorizing answers; it's about grasping the underlying principles and applying them to real-world scenarios. We hope this book serves as an invaluable tool in your journey to becoming a proficient operating systems expert.

Table of Contents

Chapter 1: Introduction to Operating Systems

What is an Operating System?

1. What is an operating system, and why is it important for a computer?

Answer: An operating system is system software that manages computer hardware, software resources, and provides essential services for computer programs. It acts as an intermediary between users and the computer hardware, enabling users to interact with the system and applications to run effectively.

2. Name a few common operating systems used today.

Answer: Common operating systems include Microsoft Windows, macOS (formerly OS X), Linux, and Unix.

3. Explain the difference between a kernel and a shell in an operating system.

Answer: The kernel is the core component of the operating system responsible for managing hardware resources, while the shell is a user interface that allows users to interact with the operating system.

4. What is multitasking in the context of operating systems?

Answer: Multitasking refers to the ability of an operating system to run multiple processes or tasks concurrently, allowing users to switch between them seamlessly.

5.Define a file system and its role within an operating system.

Answer: A file system is a method used by the operating system to organize and manage files and data on storage devices. It defines how data is stored, retrieved, and organized on the storage media.

6. What is virtual memory, and how does it benefit an operating system?

Answer: Virtual memory is a memory management technique that uses a combination of physical RAM and disk space to provide an illusion of a larger memory space. It allows running more programs than physical RAM can accommodate and provides isolation between processes.

7. Explain the concept of a process in the context of operating systems.

Answer: A process is an independent program or task managed by the operating system. Each process has its own memory space, resources, and execution context. Processes can run concurrently and communicate with each other.

8. What are system calls, and why are they important in operating systems?

Answer: System calls are interface functions that allow user-level programs to request services from the operating system, such as input/output operations, process management, and memory allocation. They are crucial for applications to interact with hardware and the OS kernel.

9. What is the difference between a 32-bit and 64-bit operating system?

Answer: The main difference is the maximum amount of memory (RAM) a system can address. A 32-bit OS can address up to 4 GB of RAM, while a 64-bit OS can handle much larger amounts of memory, providing better performance for modern computers.

10. Explain the role of device drivers in an operating system.

Answer: Device drivers are software components that facilitate communication between the operating system and hardware devices (e.g., printers, graphics cards). They translate high-level OS commands into instructions that hardware can understand, enabling devices to function correctly with the operating system.

Historical Overview

1. What was the first operating system ever created, and who developed it?

Answer: The first operating system was the "GM-NAA I/O," developed by General Motors for the UNIVAC I computer in the early 1950s.

2. Can you describe the evolution of operating systems from batch processing to time-sharing systems?

Answer: Operating systems evolved from batch processing systems, where jobs were executed in sequence, to time-sharing systems, which allowed multiple users to interact with the computer simultaneously.

3. What significant role did IBM's System/360 play in the history of operating systems?

Answer: IBM's System/360 introduced the concept of a compatible family of computers and OS/360, a unified operating system that could run on multiple hardware configurations, which was a major step in the standardization of operating systems.

4. Explain the importance of Unix in the history of operating systems.

Answer: Unix, developed in the late 1960s at AT&T Bell Labs, played a pivotal role in the development of multi-user, multitasking operating systems. It had a significant impact on subsequent OS designs and inspired many modern operating systems.

5. What is the significance of the development of graphical user interfaces (GUIs) like the Xerox Alto, Macintosh, and Windows in the history of operating systems?

Answer: GUIs revolutionized the way users interacted with computers, making them more user-friendly and accessible. The Xerox Alto, Macintosh, and Windows played crucial roles in popularizing GUIs.

6. How did the advent of personal computers in the late 20th century impact the development of operating systems?

Answer: Personal computers led to the development of user-friendly operating systems like Microsoft's MS-DOS and Windows and Apple's Macintosh System. These OSs were designed for single-user systems.

7. Discuss the transition from 32-bit to 64-bit operating systems. What benefits did 64-bit systems bring?

Answer: The transition to 64-bit operating systems allowed for larger memory addressing, which improved performance and enabled more robust and efficient applications.

8. What role did open-source operating systems, such as Linux, play in the history of operating systems?

Answer: Open-source operating systems, like Linux, fostered collaboration and innovation by allowing anyone to contribute. Linux became a prominent example of community-driven, freely available operating systems.

9. Explain the impact of mobile operating systems like iOS and Android on the computing landscape.

Answer: Mobile operating systems revolutionized personal computing by bringing powerful, user-friendly interfaces and app ecosystems to smartphones and tablets, changing the way people interact with technology.

10. What are some recent trends in operating systems, and how are they shaping the future of computing?

Answer: Recent trends include containerization, virtualization, and cloud-native operating systems. They are changing how applications are developed, deployed, and managed in a cloud-based and distributed computing environment.

Operating System Functions

1. What is the primary role of an operating system?

Answer: The primary role of an operating system is to manage computer hardware and provide services to software applications, ensuring the efficient utilization of system resources.

2. Explain the difference between process and thread in the context of an operating system.

Answer: A process is an independent program with its own memory space, while a thread is a lightweight subunit of a process that shares the same memory space. Threads within a process can execute concurrently, making them more efficient for multitasking.

3. What is the purpose of the file system in an operating system?

Answer: The file system provides a structured way to organize, store, and retrieve data on a storage device. It manages files and directories, ensuring data integrity, access control, and efficient storage.

4. What is virtual memory, and how does it work in an operating system?

Answer: Virtual memory is a memory management technique that uses a combination of physical RAM and disk space to simulate larger memory. It allows processes to access more memory than is physically available, using paging or segmentation to swap data between RAM and disk as needed.

5. Explain the concept of process scheduling.

Answer: Process scheduling is the task of selecting the next process to run on a CPU. The operating system uses scheduling algorithms to allocate CPU time to processes, ensuring fairness, efficiency, and responsiveness.

6. What are system calls, and why are they essential in operating systems?

Answer: System calls are interfaces for applications to request services from the operating system, such as file operations, process control, and I/O. They provide a secure and controlled way for applications to interact with hardware and OS services.

7. What is a deadlock in the context of operating systems, and how can it be prevented or resolved?

Answer: Deadlock is a situation where two or more processes are unable to proceed because each is waiting for a resource held by the other(s). Deadlocks can be prevented or resolved using techniques like resource allocation graphs, timeouts, or process termination.

8. Explain the role of a device driver in an operating system.

Answer: Device drivers are software components that enable communication between the operating system and hardware devices. They translate high-level OS commands into instructions that the hardware can understand and vice versa.

9. What is the difference between a monolithic kernel and a microkernel?

Answer: A monolithic kernel contains most OS functions and services in a single, large executable, whereas a microkernel minimizes the kernel's size, with many services running as separate user-space processes. Microkernels offer better modularity and fault isolation.

10. How does an operating system handle memory management and protection?

Answer: An operating system manages memory by allocating and deallocating memory blocks for processes, implementing virtual memory, and using techniques like paging and segmentation. Protection mechanisms, like memory access permissions, prevent one process from accessing or modifying the memory of another process.

Types of Operating Systems

1. What are the primary types of operating systems, and can you briefly describe each?

Answer: The primary types of operating systems are:

Single-User, Single-Tasking

Single-User, Multi-Tasking

Multi-User

Real-Time

Network

2. What is the key distinction between a single-user, single-tasking operating system and a single-user, multi-tasking operating system?

Answer: A single-user, single-tasking OS allows only one task to run at a time, while a single-user, multi-tasking OS permits multiple tasks to run concurrently, switching between them to give the illusion of parallel execution.

3. Explain the significance of multi-user operating systems.

Answer: Multi-user operating systems allow multiple users to access and use a computer system simultaneously. They provide user account management, resource allocation, and security features to ensure user isolation.

4. What are the characteristics of a real-time operating system, and in what applications are they commonly used?

Answer: Real-time operating systems are designed to provide predictable and consistent response times. They are commonly used in applications like aircraft control systems, medical equipment, and industrial automation.

5. How does a network operating system differ from other types of operating systems?

Answer: A network operating system is designed to manage and coordinate network resources, allowing multiple devices to communicate and share resources. It focuses on network protocols, file sharing, and access control.

6. What challenges and considerations are specific to multi-user operating systems compared to single-user systems?

Answer: Multi-user systems must handle issues like user authentication, resource sharing, and concurrent access, and implement security measures to protect data and maintain user separation.

7. Can you give an example of a single-user, single-tasking operating system and describe a scenario where it might be used?

Answer: An example is MS-DOS. It might be used in embedded systems where only a single, specific function needs to be performed, like in an industrial control system.

8. What are the key features that distinguish a real-time operating system from other types in terms of task scheduling and responsiveness?

Answer: Real-time OSs use priority-based scheduling, ensuring that critical tasks get executed on time. They provide low and deterministic response times, crucial in time-sensitive applications.

9. What is the primary role of a network operating system in managing resources and communication within a networked environment?

Answer: A network operating system manages file sharing, user authentication, network protocols, and access control to enable devices on a network to share resources and communicate efficiently.

10. In which scenarios would you recommend the use of a single-user, multi-tasking operating system over a multi-user operating system, and why?

Answer: Single-user, multi-tasking OSs are suitable for personal computers, where a single user needs to run multiple applications concurrently. They are simpler and more resource-efficient compared to multi-user systems, which may be overkill for single users.

Needs of Operating Systems

1. Why is an operating system necessary for a computer system?

Answer: An operating system is essential as it acts as an intermediary between hardware and software, managing resources and providing a user-friendly interface for users and applications.

2. What are the primary functions of an operating system and why are they important?

Answer: The primary functions include process management, memory management, file system management, device management, and user interface. These functions are critical for resource allocation, stability, and security of the computer system.

3. How does an operating system facilitate hardware resource management, and why is this crucial?

Answer: Operating systems allocate and control hardware resources, ensuring fair and efficient utilization, preventing conflicts, and maximizing system performance.

4. Explain the role of process management in an operating system and why it's needed.

Answer: Process management involves creating, scheduling, and terminating processes. It's crucial for multitasking, resource allocation, and maintaining system responsiveness.

5. What is the significance of memory management in an operating system, and how does it prevent issues like memory leaks or overutilization?

Answer: Memory management ensures efficient memory allocation, prevents memory leaks, and protects one process from accessing another's memory space. It's essential for system stability.

6. Why is file system management necessary, and how does an operating system provide a structured way to store and retrieve data?

Answer: File system management ensures data organization, access control, and integrity. Operating systems offer file systems to manage and structure data storage.

7. How does an operating system handle device management, and why is it important for user applications and system stability?

Answer: Device management controls hardware devices, enabling user applications to interact with them. It ensures device access is secure, reliable, and prevents conflicts.

8. Discuss the role of user interface in operating systems and its impact on user experience.

Answer: The user interface provides a means for users to interact with the computer. A well-designed interface enhances user experience, making computing tasks more accessible and user-friendly.

9. Why is security a critical need in operating systems, and how does it address issues like unauthorized access and data protection?

Answer: Security is crucial to protect data and prevent unauthorized access. Operating systems implement authentication, access controls, encryption, and other security measures.

10. In what scenarios might a computer not require a traditional operating system, and what alternatives could be used?

Answer: In embedded systems or specialized devices with limited functionality, a traditional operating system may not be necessary. These systems may use a real-time OS or firmware to fulfill their specific requirements.

Spooling and Buffering

1. What is spooling, and how does it work in computing?

Answer: Spooling stands for "Simultaneous Peripheral Operation On-Line." It is a technique that allows multiple processes to use input and output devices efficiently by placing data in a queue, which the device can access as it becomes available.

2. Why is spooling essential in operating systems, and what benefits does it provide?

Answer: Spooling is crucial for managing input and output operations in a way that prevents processes from waiting for devices to become available. It improves system throughput and minimizes idle time.

3. Can you explain the difference between input spooling and output spooling?

Answer: Input spooling involves queuing data from input devices (e.g., keyboards) for later processing, while output spooling queues data from processes for output devices (e.g., printers) to handle.

4. What are the primary components of a spooling system, and how do they work together?

Answer: A spooling system consists of a spooler, a disk or spooling directory, and the I/O devices. The spooler manages the queue, while the disk stores spooled data, and I/O devices read from or write to the spooling directory.

5. What challenges might be encountered when implementing spooling, and how can they be mitigated?

Answer: Challenges include managing the spooling directory's size, handling priority of different jobs, and ensuring data integrity. These issues can be addressed through proper directory management and job prioritization.

6. What is buffering in the context of data transmission and storage?

Answer: Buffering involves temporarily storing data in a buffer (a memory area) to balance data transfer rates between two devices or processes with mismatched speeds.

7. How does buffering contribute to data transfer efficiency and prevention of data loss?

Answer: Buffering allows for smoother data transfer by temporarily storing data until the receiving side can process it. This prevents data loss due to speed disparities.

8. What is the key difference between input buffering and output buffering?

Answer: Input buffering stores incoming data before it's processed, while output buffering stores data that has been processed but not yet sent to the destination.

9. Explain the concept of double buffering and its applications.

Answer: Double buffering involves using two buffers in a cyclical manner, allowing data to be continuously transferred between them. This is often used in multimedia applications, gaming, and graphics to eliminate flickering or tearing.

10. What are the potential drawbacks of buffering, and how can they be mitigated?

Answer: Buffering can lead to increased memory usage and latency. Mitigation involves careful management of buffer size and ensuring that buffers are emptied or refilled efficiently to avoid data overload or long delays.

Spooling over Buffering

1. What is the primary purpose of spooling, and how does it differ from buffering?

Answer: Spooling is primarily used to manage and queue data for input/output devices, allowing multiple processes to use them efficiently. Buffering, on the other hand, temporarily stores data to balance the speed difference between producers and consumers.

2. How does spooling contribute to efficient device utilization, and how does it compare to buffering in this aspect?

Answer: Spooling enhances device utilization by queuing tasks, reducing device idle time. Buffering, while reducing data transfer bottlenecks, focuses on maintaining a continuous data flow between two components.

3. Can you describe a scenario where spooling would be more advantageous than buffering, and why?

Answer: Spooling is advantageous when multiple processes share a single device (e.g., a printer), ensuring fairness and preventing processes from waiting. Buffering may not be as effective in such scenarios.

4. What challenges might be faced when implementing spooling, and how do these differ from challenges faced in buffering?

Answer: Challenges in spooling may include managing a spooling directory and handling job priorities. Buffering challenges are typically related to buffer size and data synchronization between producers and consumers.

5. Explain the role of spooling in managing printer tasks and why buffering might not be as effective in this context.

Answer: Spooling manages print jobs in a queue, ensuring that multiple print tasks can be executed sequentially. Buffering may not guarantee that print jobs are processed in the order they were received.

6. What are the key advantages of spooling in a multi-user environment?

Answer: Spooling prevents processes from waiting for shared devices, ensuring efficient resource utilization, minimizing idle time, and allowing for orderly processing of tasks.

7. How does spooling enhance the reliability of data processing and device access in a computer system?

Answer: Spooling helps prevent data loss and device contention by providing a structured queue system, ensuring each process has its turn to access the device.

8. In what situations is spooling particularly beneficial for managing data processing and device access?

Answer: Spooling is highly beneficial when multiple users or processes share limited resources like printers, ensuring fair and orderly access to the device.

Buffering Advantages Questions:

1. What are the primary advantages of buffering in the context of data transmission and storage?

Answer: Buffering balances data transfer speeds between producers and consumers, preventing data loss due to speed disparities and enhancing the efficiency of data transfer.

2. Can you provide examples of scenarios where buffering is crucial for maintaining data flow and preventing bottlenecks?

Answer: Buffering is essential in multimedia streaming, network communication, and in situations where data producers and consumers operate at different speeds, such as reading from a slow disk and writing to a fast network connection.

Objective of Operating System

1. What is the primary objective of an operating system?

Answer: The primary objective of an operating system is to provide an environment in which computer hardware and software can interact efficiently, managing resources and providing services to users and applications.

2. How does an operating system achieve the objective of resource allocation?

Answer: An operating system allocates resources such as CPU time, memory, and I/O devices to processes and ensures fair and efficient utilization by employing scheduling and management algorithms.

3. What role does the operating system play in providing a user-friendly interface, and why is this an important objective?

Answer: The operating system provides a user-friendly interface to enable users and applications to interact with the computer system. This is essential to make computing accessible and efficient.

4. Explain the objective of process management in an operating system.

Answer: The objective of process management is to create, schedule, and terminate processes, ensuring that multiple tasks can run concurrently while maintaining system stability.

5. Why is data security an important objective of an operating system, and how does it achieve this goal?

Answer: Data security is crucial to protect user data and system resources. The operating system enforces access controls, encryption, and authentication mechanisms to achieve this objective.

6. What is the significance of memory management as an objective in operating systems, and how does it help in optimizing system performance?

Answer: Memory management ensures efficient allocation and protection of memory, preventing issues like memory leaks and optimizing system performance by minimizing fragmentation.

7. How does the objective of I/O device management benefit a computer system, and what challenges does it address?

Answer: I/O device management allows efficient and controlled access to devices, preventing resource contention, ensuring reliable data transfer, and addressing device synchronization challenges.

8. What role does the operating system play in achieving the objective of file system management, and why is it essential?

Answer: File system management organizes and maintains data on storage devices. The operating system provides file operations, access controls, and data integrity to ensure efficient storage and retrieval of data.

9. Why is fault tolerance and error handling an objective in operating systems, and how does it enhance system reliability?

Answer: The objective of fault tolerance and error handling is to ensure that the system can continue operating in the presence of errors or failures. It enhances system reliability by providing mechanisms to recover from faults.

10. How does the operating system's objective of resource abstraction and virtualization simplify the interaction between hardware and software?

Answer: Resource abstraction and virtualization hide hardware complexities from applications, allowing software to interact with resources in a consistent and user-friendly manner. This simplifies software development and enhances portability.

ONLINE RESOURCES

Practice Paper Link : https://forms.gle/PCJTE9PduHKzzGew9

QR Code :

Video Link : https://www.youtube.com/playlist?list=PLzlh_31VWEFqv1VgO4t3ClJJUIWrFeGU7

QR Code :

Chapter 2: Computer System Structures

Computer Hardware Overview

1. What is computer hardware, and how does it differ from software?

Answer: Computer hardware refers to the physical components of a computer system, such as the CPU, memory, and storage devices. Software, on the other hand, includes programs and instructions that run on the hardware.

2. Can you name some essential hardware components of a typical computer system?

Answer: Essential hardware components include the central processing unit (CPU), memory (RAM), storage devices (hard drive, SSD), motherboard, graphics card, and input/output devices (keyboard, mouse, monitor).

3. Explain the role of the central processing unit (CPU) in a computer system.

Answer: The CPU is the brain of the computer, responsible for executing instructions and performing calculations. It fetches, decodes, and executes instructions from programs and controls other hardware components.

4. What is the purpose of memory (RAM) in a computer, and how does it differ from storage devices like hard drives?

Answer: RAM (Random Access Memory) provides temporary storage for data and programs that are actively in use. It is faster but volatile, meaning it loses data when the computer is powered off. In contrast, storage devices provide long-term, non-volatile data storage.

5. How do storage devices like hard drives and SSDs work, and what are their key differences?

Answer: Both hard drives and SSDs store data, but hard drives use spinning disks and read/write heads, while SSDs use flash memory. SSDs are faster, more durable, and consume less power compared to hard drives.

6. What is the function of the motherboard in a computer system, and why is it important?

Answer: The motherboard is the main circuit board that connects and coordinates all hardware components. It provides pathways for data and power, houses the CPU, and facilitates communication between components.

7. Explain the role of the graphics card (GPU) in a computer and its significance, especially for gaming and multimedia applications.

Answer: The graphics card is responsible for rendering graphics and videos. It offloads graphical processing from the CPU, making it crucial for gaming and multimedia applications by improving performance and visual quality.

8 What are input/output (I/O) devices, and can you provide examples of commonly used I/O devices?

Answer: I/O devices allow users to input data into the computer and receive output. Common examples include keyboards, mice, monitors, printers, and external storage devices.

9. How does the concept of computer architecture relate to hardware design, and why is it important for system performance?

Answer: Computer architecture refers to the design of a computer system's hardware components and their interconnections. It impacts performance, scalability, and compatibility with software and applications.

10. Why is understanding computer hardware essential for computer science professionals, and how does it benefit troubleshooting and optimization?

Answer: A deep understanding of computer hardware is crucial for computer science professionals as it enables effective troubleshooting, optimization, and development of software and applications that fully utilize the capabilities of the underlying hardware.

Operating System Services

1. What are operating system services, and why are they essential for computer systems?

Answer: Operating system services are a set of functions that provide an interface between hardware and software, managing resources and offering services to applications. They are essential for resource allocation, security, and efficient software execution.

2. Can you explain the difference between system calls and application programming interfaces (APIs) in the context of operating system services?

Answer: System calls are functions provided by the operating system that applications use to request services, whereas APIs are sets of functions and routines that applications use to access system resources and services.

3. What is process management as an operating system service, and how does it benefit multitasking and resource utilization?

Answer: Process management involves creating, scheduling, and terminating processes. It allows multitasking by giving each process a fair share of CPU time, optimizing resource utilization.

4. How does memory management as an operating system service prevent memory fragmentation and ensure efficient use of system memory?

Answer: Memory management allocates and deallocates memory, preventing fragmentation and ensuring that processes can efficiently use available memory, improving overall system performance.

5. Explain the importance of file system services, and how do they contribute to data organization and access control?

Answer: File system services help organize data on storage devices, control access to files, and ensure data integrity, making data storage and retrieval efficient and secure.

6. What role does I/O device management play in ensuring smooth interaction between applications and hardware devices, and how does it improve system reliability?

Answer: I/O device management handles device access, preventing resource contention and ensuring reliable data transfer, which is critical for system reliability and efficient I/O operations.

7. Why is the security and protection service important for an operating system, and what measures does it implement to safeguard the system and its resources?

Answer: Security and protection services enforce access controls, authentication, encryption, and other security measures to protect the system and its resources from unauthorized access and malicious threats.

8. Explain the role of network and communication services in operating systems and their importance in modern computing environments.

Answer: Network and communication services facilitate data exchange between computers and across networks. They are crucial for modern computing, enabling internet connectivity, data sharing, and remote access.

9. How do utility programs provided by the operating system enhance user experience and system maintenance?

Answer: Utility programs, like text editors, disk maintenance tools, and system diagnostic programs, enhance user experience by providing tools for data manipulation, system optimization, and troubleshooting.

10. In what ways does the operating system fulfill the objective of providing a user-friendly interface, and how does this interface impact the user's interaction with the system?

Answer: The operating system offers graphical user interfaces (GUIs) and command-line interfaces (CLIs) that allow users to interact with the system through intuitive controls or commands, simplifying tasks and improving user productivity.

System Calls

1. What is a system call, and how does it differ from a regular function call in a program?

Answer: A system call is a request for a service provided by the operating system, typically involving tasks like I/O operations, process management, or resource allocation. It differs from a regular function call as it involves a transition from user mode to kernel mode, where the operating system performs the requested task.

2. Why are system calls necessary for applications and the operating system?

Answer: System calls provide a controlled and secure interface for applications to access operating system services. They allow applications to perform tasks like file I/O, process management, and memory allocation while maintaining system stability and security.

3. What are the common categories of system calls, and can you give examples of system calls in each category?

Answer: Common categories include process control (e.g., fork, exec), file management (e.g., open, read, write), device management (e.g., read, write, ioctl), information maintenance (e.g., getpid, time), and communication (e.g., socket, send, receive).

4. How does a system call transition from user mode to kernel mode, and what role does the system call interface play in this process?

Answer: A system call is invoked through the system call interface, which triggers a trap or interrupt. The hardware then switches the CPU from user mode to kernel mode, and the operating system handles the system call.

5. Explain the significance of system call error codes and how they are used by applications to handle errors.

Answer: System call error codes indicate the success or failure of a system call. Applications can check error codes to handle exceptions or errors gracefully, such as by retrying or displaying an error message.

6. What is the relationship between system calls and libraries in programming, and how do libraries simplify application development?

Answer: Libraries often encapsulate system calls, providing higher-level functions that make application development easier and more portable. Applications use library functions, which internally invoke the necessary system calls.

7. Why is system call performance critical for the overall performance of an application or system, and what factors can impact system call efficiency?

Answer: System call performance is crucial because system calls are often the bottleneck in application execution. Factors affecting efficiency include the frequency of system calls, the design of the operating system, and the underlying hardware.

8. What is the purpose of the fork system call, and how does it enable the creation of new processes in Unix-like operating systems?

Answer: The fork system call creates a new process that is a copy of the calling process. This new process can execute different code and share the same memory space. It is the basis for process creation in Unix-like systems.

9. Can you explain how file-related system calls like open, read, and write are used by applications, and why they are crucial for data handling?

Answer: open is used to access files, while read and write are used to read from and write to files. These system calls enable applications to perform I/O operations on files, facilitating data handling.

10. How do system calls facilitate communication between processes in an operating system, and can you provide examples of communication-related system calls?

Answer: System calls like pipe, socket, send, and receive enable inter-process communication (IPC). For example, socket is used for network communication, and pipe allows communication between processes on the same system.

System Programs

1. What are system programs, and how do they differ from application programs?

Answer: System programs are software components that provide various services and utilities to the operating system and users. They differ from application programs in that they interact more closely with the operating system and manage system resources.

2. Can you explain the role of system utilities in a computer system, and provide examples of common system utilities?

Answer: System utilities are system programs that perform various maintenance, administrative, and diagnostic tasks. Examples include file management utilities, disk cleanup tools, and performance monitoring programs.

3. Why are file management programs considered essential system utilities, and how do they help users organize and access their data?

Answer: File management programs help users organize, manipulate, and access their files and directories efficiently, providing tools like file creation, copying, moving, and searching.

4. What is the purpose of system diagnostics and debugging tools, and how do they assist system administrators and developers?

Answer: System diagnostic and debugging tools help identify and resolve system issues and software bugs. They assist administrators and developers in troubleshooting and optimizing system performance.

5. Explain the role of antivirus software and firewall programs as system utilities, and why they are crucial for system security.

Answer: Antivirus software scans for and removes malware, while firewall programs monitor and control network traffic. They are essential system utilities for safeguarding the system against security threats.

6. How do backup and recovery utilities help users and organizations protect their data and maintain business continuity?

Answer: Backup and recovery utilities create copies of important data, allowing users to recover data in case of accidental deletion or hardware failures. They are crucial for data protection and disaster recovery.

7. What is the purpose of system call tracing and monitoring tools, and how do they aid in performance analysis and debugging?

Answer: System call tracing and monitoring tools record system calls made by programs, helping in performance analysis and debugging by identifying bottlenecks, resource usage, and application behaviour.

8. Can you describe system initialization and shutdown procedures and explain the role of boot loaders in the start-up process?

Answer: System initialization procedures prepare the system for use, and shutdown procedures ensure a safe system shutdown. Boot loaders are responsible for loading the operating system into memory during start-up.

9. How do system configuration and management tools assist administrators in setting up and maintaining system parameters, such as user accounts and network configurations?

Answer: System configuration and management tools allow administrators to configure and control system parameters, user accounts, and network settings, simplifying system administration tasks.

10. Explain the significance of text editors and command interpreters as system programs, and how they enhance user interaction with the operating system.

Answer: Text editors allow users to create and edit text files, while command interpreters provide a command-line interface for interacting with the operating system. They enhance user interaction by providing flexibility and control over system operations.

Operating System Structure

1. What is the structure of an operating system, and why is it important to understand it?

Answer: The structure of an operating system represents its organization and design. Understanding it is vital for comprehending how different components interact and for efficient development and maintenance.

2. Explain the concept of a monolithic kernel and its key characteristics.

Answer: A monolithic kernel is a single, large program that manages all OS functions and services. It combines various components like process management, file system, and device drivers into one executable.

3. What is the difference between a monolithic kernel and a microkernel in terms of structure and design?

Answer: A monolithic kernel integrates all OS functions in a single executable, whereas a microkernel minimizes the kernel's size by separating services into user-space processes. Microkernels offer better modularity and fault isolation.

4. Can you describe the layered structure of some operating systems and explain how it simplifies design and maintenance?

Answer: Layered structures organize the OS into distinct layers, with each layer relying only on the layers below it. This separation simplifies design, maintenance, and the addition of new features.

5. What is a client-server model in the context of operating system structure, and how does it enhance modularity and scalability?

Answer: In a client-server model, the OS is divided into servers that provide services and clients that request them. This promotes modularity, scalability, and the ability to add new services without affecting existing ones.

6. Explain the significance of system calls and their role in the structure of an operating system.

Answer: System calls provide an interface for applications to request services from the OS. They are a crucial part of the OS structure as they allow software to interact with hardware and OS services.

7. How does the structure of a microkernel-based operating system contribute to reliability and fault tolerance?

Answer: A microkernel isolates services in separate processes, reducing the impact of faults in one service on others. This enhances reliability and fault tolerance.

8. Describe the concept of a hybrid kernel in operating system design, and how does it combine features from both monolithic and microkernel structures?

Answer: A hybrid kernel combines the efficiency of monolithic kernels with the modularity of microkernels. It keeps core services in the kernel while moving non-core services to user space, offering a balance between performance and flexibility.

9. What is the role of the shell in the structure of an operating system, and how does it enhance user interaction with the OS?

Answer: The shell is the command-line interface that enables users to communicate with the OS. It interprets user commands and interacts with the kernel to execute them, facilitating user interaction with the system.

10. Explain the concept of loadable kernel modules and their importance in the structure of modern operating systems.

Answer: Loadable kernel modules are pieces of code that can be dynamically loaded and unloaded into the kernel. They enhance the OS structure by allowing the addition of new functionality without recompiling the entire kernel.

Virtual Machines

1. What is a virtual machine (VM), and how does it differ from a physical machine?

Answer: A virtual machine is a software-based emulation of a physical computer, running an operating system and applications. It differs from a physical machine in that it operates within a host system and shares its resources.

2. What are the primary advantages of using virtual machines in computing environments?

Answer: Virtual machines offer benefits such as hardware consolidation, improved resource utilization, isolation, ease of management, and support for legacy software.

3. Explain the concept of host and guest operating systems in the context of virtual machines.

Answer: The host operating system is the OS of the physical machine, while the guest operating system runs inside the virtual machine. The host manages VM resources and facilitates their operation.

4. What role does a hypervisor play in managing virtual machines, and can you differentiate between Type 1 and Type 2 hypervisors?

Answer: A hypervisor is a software layer that manages and controls virtual machines. Type 1 hypervisors run directly on the physical hardware, while Type 2 hypervisors run on top of an existing operating system.

5. How does virtualization impact resource allocation and sharing among multiple virtual machines on a single physical host?

Answer: Virtualization enables efficient resource sharing by allowing multiple VMs to run concurrently on a single physical machine. The hypervisor allocates resources and ensures isolation between VMs.

6. What are the use cases for virtualization, and how does it benefit businesses and organizations?

Answer: Virtualization is used for server consolidation, development and testing environments, disaster recovery, and cloud computing. It reduces hardware costs, enhances flexibility, and streamlines resource management.

7. Explain the term "snapshot" in the context of virtual machines, and how does it assist in backup and recovery processes?

Answer: A snapshot is a point-in-time copy of a virtual machine's state. It is used to back up and recover VMs, allowing users to return to a specific state in case of issues or data loss.

8. How does live migration work in virtualization, and what is its importance in ensuring continuous service availability?

Answer: Live migration allows a running VM to be moved from one physical host to another without service interruption. It's essential for load balancing, resource maintenance, and avoiding downtime.

9. Discuss the concept of containerization, and how does it differ from virtualization using VMs?

Answer: Containerization is a lightweight form of virtualization that runs applications and their dependencies in isolated containers. Unlike VMs, containers share the host OS, making them more efficient and portable.

10. What security considerations are relevant to virtual machines, and how can organizations ensure the security of their virtualized environments?

Answer: Security concerns include VM escape attacks, data leakage, and VM sprawl. Organizations can enhance security through regular patching, network segmentation, access controls, and monitoring.

ONLINE RESOURCES

Practice Paper Link : https://forms.gle/gxUAA4m5gFtU4hdX6

QR Code :

Video Link: https://www.youtube.com/playlist?list=PLzlh_31VWEFqxHZkYsZ6Xy_dFG4IHwBDg

QR Code :

Chapter 3: Process Management

Processes and Threads

1. What is a process in the context of operating systems, and how does it differ from a thread?

Answer: A process is an independent program with its own memory space and resources, while a thread is a lightweight unit of execution within a process that shares the same memory and resources. Processes are independent of each other, while threads within the same process can communicate more efficiently.

2. Explain the concept of a process control block (PCB) and its role in process management.

Answer: A PCB is a data structure that contains information about a process, such as its state, program counter, and registers. It is used by the operating system to manage and switch between processes.

3. What is the purpose of process scheduling, and how does it improve system efficiency in a multitasking environment?

Answer: Process scheduling is the allocation of CPU time to processes. It improves system efficiency by ensuring fair CPU time distribution, responsiveness, and efficient resource utilization.

4. Can you describe the concept of a thread and explain the advantages of using multithreading in applications?

Answer: A thread is a lightweight unit of execution within a process. Multithreading enhances application responsiveness and performance by allowing multiple threads to run concurrently and share resources.

5. How do threads within the same process communicate and share data, and what synchronization mechanisms are commonly used to avoid conflicts?

Answer: Threads within the same process can communicate and share data through shared memory. Synchronization mechanisms like mutexes, semaphores, and condition variables are used to prevent data conflicts and ensure safe access.

6. Explain the concept of a parent process and child process, and how they are related in process creation.

Answer: A parent process can create child processes, which inherit some of the parent's attributes. The parent is typically responsible for managing and monitoring the child processes.

7. What is the role of the process state diagram in visualizing the life cycle of a process, and what are the main states a process can be in?

Answer: The process state diagram illustrates the life cycle of a process, including states such as new, ready, running, waiting, terminated, and more. It provides a visual representation of a process's progress.

8. How can race conditions and data corruption be prevented in multithreaded applications, and what are some common synchronization techniques?

Answer: Race conditions and data corruption can be prevented through synchronization techniques such as locks, semaphores, and barriers. These mechanisms ensure that threads access shared resources safely and in a coordinated manner.

9. What is the significance of context switching in the execution of processes and threads, and how does it impact system performance?

Answer: Context switching involves saving the state of one process or thread and restoring the state of another. It is essential for multitasking but introduces some overhead, impacting system performance.

10. Explain the concept of thread priority and how it influences thread execution within a process.

Answer: Thread priority determines the order in which threads within a process are scheduled to run. Threads with higher priority are given precedence over lower-priority threads, allowing for more control over execution.

Process States

1. What are process states, and how do they relate to multitasking in an operating system?

Answer: Process states represent the different stages a process goes through in its lifecycle within an operating system. These states are typically "Running," "Ready," "Blocked," and "Terminated." Multitasking is achieved by allowing the operating system to switch between these states to efficiently utilize the CPU and execute multiple processes concurrently.

2. Explain the differences between the "Ready" and "Running" process states.

Answer: The "Ready" state is when a process is loaded into memory and is waiting for its turn to execute. In contrast, the "Running" state indicates that the CPU is actively executing the instructions of the process. Processes transition from "Ready" to "Running" when the CPU scheduler allocates CPU time to them.

3. What causes a process to transition from the "Running" state to the "Blocked" state?

Answer: A process enters the "Blocked" state when it needs to wait for an external event, such as I/O operations (e.g., reading from disk) or user input. While blocked, the process is not utilizing the CPU, allowing other processes to run.

4. How does the operating system manage process states during context switching?

Answer: During a context switch, the operating system saves the current state of the running process, changes its state to "Ready," and selects a new process in the "Ready" state to execute. It then loads the state of the newly selected process and changes its state to "Running."

5. Explain what a zombie process is and how it relates to process states.

Answer: A zombie process is a process that has completed its execution but has not yet been fully removed from the process table. It is in a terminated state but still has an entry in the process table until its parent process acknowledges its termination and releases its resources.

6. Can a process transition directly from the "Blocked" state to the "Running" state? If so, under what circumstances?

Answer: Yes, a process can transition from the "Blocked" state to the "Running" state when the event it was waiting for (e.g., completion of I/O) occurs. This transition is managed by the operating system to ensure that processes resume execution when their dependencies are met.

7. How does the concept of process priority affect process states and scheduling?

Answer: Process priority influences the order in which processes in the "Ready" state are selected to run. Higher-priority processes are typically scheduled to run before lower-priority ones. This prioritization can impact the distribution of CPU time among processes in the "Running" state.

8. What is a race condition in the context of process states, and how can it be mitigated?

Answer: A race condition occurs when the behaviour of a program depends on the relative timing of events, such as process state changes. It can lead to unexpected and undesired results. To mitigate race conditions, synchronization mechanisms like locks, semaphores, and mutexes are used to ensure that processes access shared resources in a controlled manner.

9. Explain how a process can be suspended and what the implications are for its state.

Answer: A process can be suspended by the operating system, which effectively pauses its execution. The process state is typically changed to "Suspended." This is done to free up resources or manage resource conflicts. When a process is suspended, it is not allowed to execute until it is resumed.

10. What are the advantages of using a multi-threaded approach within a process in terms of process states and performance?

Answer: Multi-threading allows a process to have multiple threads of execution, each with its own set of registers and stack. This can improve performance by allowing parallel execution and efficient resource sharing among threads within the same process. Threads in a multi-threaded process can be managed more flexibly as they share the same process state, making context switches between them faster and more efficient.

Process Scheduling

1. What is process scheduling, and why is it essential in an operating system?

Answer: Process scheduling is the mechanism by which the operating system decides which process to execute next on the CPU. It is essential for efficient resource utilization and to provide the illusion of multitasking, enabling multiple processes to run concurrently.

2. Explain the difference between pre-emptive and non-pre-emptive scheduling. Give examples of each.

Answer: Pre-emptive scheduling allows the operating system to interrupt and switch to another process while it's executing. Non-pre-emptive (or cooperative) scheduling relies on processes voluntarily giving up the CPU. An example of pre-emptive scheduling is the Round Robin algorithm, while an example of non-pre-emptive scheduling is First-Come-First-Serve (FCFS).

3. What are the criteria used to evaluate the effectiveness of a scheduling algorithm?

Answer: Scheduling algorithms are evaluated based on criteria like CPU utilization, throughput, turnaround time, waiting time, response time, and fairness. The effectiveness of an algorithm depends on how well it optimizes these factors.

4. Describe the Round Robin scheduling algorithm and its advantages and disadvantages.

Answer: Round Robin assigns each process a fixed time quantum for execution. It's simple and ensures fairness. However, it can lead to high context switch overhead, and short processes may wait longer if long processes hold the CPU.

5. What is priority scheduling, and how can it be prone to starvation?

Answer: Priority scheduling assigns priorities to processes, with higher priority processes executed first. Starvation can occur when low-priority processes never get a chance to run if high-priority processes are continually arriving.

6. Explain the concept of aging in relation to priority scheduling.

Answer: Aging is a technique in priority scheduling that gradually increases the priority of a process as it waits in the ready queue. This ensures that long-waiting processes don't starve and eventually get their turn to run.

7. What is the critical section problem, and how can process scheduling algorithms help address it?

Answer: The critical section problem is about processes safely accessing shared resources without interference. Scheduling algorithms can help by ensuring that only one process can access the critical section at a time, preventing data corruption.

8. Discuss the advantages and disadvantages of the Shortest Job First (SJF) scheduling algorithm.

Answer: SJF minimizes waiting time and turnaround time for processes with shorter burst times. However, it's challenging to predict the exact burst times, and its pre-emptive version can lead to frequent context switches.

9. What is the difference between a multilevel queue and a multilevel feedback queue scheduling algorithm?

Answer: A multilevel queue has multiple queues with different priorities, and each queue follows a different scheduling algorithm. In a multilevel feedback queue, processes can move between queues based on their behaviour, allowing dynamic adjustment of priorities.

10. Explain the concept of in-order execution and out-of-order execution in process scheduling.

Answer: In-order execution follows the order in which processes are placed in the ready queue. Out-of-order execution allows the scheduler to select processes out of sequence based on their priority, which can lead to better system responsiveness and throughput.

Interprocess Communication

1. What is interprocess communication (IPC), and why is it important in operating systems?

Answer: IPC refers to the methods and mechanisms that processes use to communicate and share data with each other. It's crucial for processes to collaborate, exchange information, and synchronize their actions in a multitasking operating system.

2. Explain the differences between message passing and shared memory as IPC mechanisms.

Answer: Message passing involves processes sending messages to each other through the operating system, while shared memory allows processes to share a common region of memory. Message passing is typically safer and more straightforward, while shared memory offers higher performance.

3. What are some common problems that can arise in IPC, and how can they be mitigated?

Answer: Common IPC problems include race conditions, deadlocks, and data consistency issues. These can be mitigated using synchronization mechanisms like locks, semaphores, and proper design of IPC protocols.

4. Describe the producer-consumer problem and how IPC can be used to solve it.

Answer: The producer-consumer problem involves one or more processes producing data and others consuming it. IPC mechanisms like semaphores or mutexes can be used to ensure that producers and consumers do not access the shared buffer simultaneously, avoiding data corruption.

5. What is a semaphore, and how does it facilitate process synchronization in IPC?

Answer: A semaphore is a synchronization mechanism used for process coordination. It provides atomic operations to control access to shared resources, preventing race conditions and ensuring mutual exclusion.

6. Explain the concept of a socket in IPC, and how is it commonly used in network communication?

Answer: A socket is an endpoint for sending or receiving data across a network. It allows processes on different machines to communicate by establishing connections and exchanging data using various socket types like TCP and UDP.

7. What is a message queue, and how does it differ from a pipe in IPC?

Answer: A message queue is a form of IPC that allows processes to send and receive messages. It is more structured and can be used for communication between unrelated processes. Pipes are unidirectional and typically used for communication between related processes.

8. Discuss the role of signals in IPC and how they are used to notify processes of events.

Answer: Signals are a form of asynchronous communication used to notify processes of events or exceptions. They can be used for tasks like handling interrupts, terminating processes, or notifying about specific conditions (e.g., the arrival of data).

9. What is remote procedure call (RPC), and how does it enable IPC between processes on different machines?

Answer: RPC is a mechanism that allows processes to invoke functions or procedures in remote processes, as if they were local. It abstracts the complexities of inter-machine communication, making it appear as a regular function call.

10. Explain the concept of a named pipe (FIFO) and its applications in IPC.

Answer: A named pipe, or FIFO, is a special file that allows processes to communicate by reading and writing to it. Named pipes are often used for interprocess communication when processes need to exchange data, especially when they are not directly related, using a common file-like interface.

Process Synchronization

1. Explain the difference between mutual exclusion and deadlock in the context of process synchronization.

Answer: Mutual exclusion ensures that only one process can access a critical section at a time. Deadlock, on the other hand, occurs when two or more processes are unable to proceed because each is waiting for a resource that another has.

2. Describe the concept of a semaphore and how it can be used for process synchronization.

Answer: A semaphore is an integer variable used for process synchronization. It provides atomic operations for controlling access to shared resources and allows for both mutual exclusion and signalling among processes.

3. What is the dining philosophers problem, and how can it be solved using synchronization mechanisms?

Answer: The dining philosophers problem is a classic synchronization problem where multiple philosophers compete for limited resources (forks). It can be solved using mutexes or semaphores to ensure that philosophers pick up the forks in a coordinated manner, avoiding deadlock.

4. Explain the difference between busy-waiting and blocking in the context of synchronization.

Answer: Busy-waiting involves repeatedly checking for a condition to be true in a loop, consuming CPU time. Blocking, on the other hand, suspends a process until a condition is met, allowing the CPU to be used more efficiently.

5. What is a condition variable, and how does it support efficient process synchronization?

Answer: A condition variable is a synchronization primitive that allows processes to wait for a specific condition to be met before proceeding. It is used in conjunction with mutexes to avoid busy-waiting and enable efficient synchronization.

6. Discuss the reader-writer problem and how it can be addressed using synchronization techniques.

Answer: The reader-writer problem involves multiple processes reading and writing to a shared resource. It can be addressed using synchronization mechanisms like semaphores or locks, with different strategies for readers and writers to ensure data consistency.

7. Explain the concept of a monitor in process synchronization, and how it simplifies the development of synchronized code.

Answer: A monitor is a higher-level abstraction that combines data, procedures, and synchronization mechanisms into a single unit. It simplifies the development of synchronized code by encapsulating the synchronization details, making it easier to reason about and maintain concurrent programs.

Peterson's Algorithm in Process Synchronization

1. What is Peterson's Algorithm, and what is its primary purpose in process synchronization?

Answer: Peterson's Algorithm is a software-based solution for achieving mutual exclusion among two processes. Its primary purpose is to ensure that only one process can enter its critical section at a time.

2. Why is Peterson's Algorithm primarily used for two processes?

Answer: Peterson's Algorithm is specifically designed for scenarios with exactly two processes. It utilizes two variables and is not easily scalable for more processes.

3. Explain the two key variables used in Peterson's Algorithm and their significance.

Answer: Peterson's Algorithm uses two variables: flag and turn. The flag variable indicates a process's desire to enter the critical section, while the turn variable designates whose turn it is to enter the critical section.

4. How does Peterson's Algorithm guarantee mutual exclusion for two processes?

Answer: Mutual exclusion is ensured in Peterson's Algorithm through the careful coordination of the flag and turn variables. Before entering the critical section, each process sets its flag to indicate its intent and checks the flag of the other process and the turn variable to determine whose turn it is. If a process determines it is not its turn or the other process has declared its intent to enter the critical section, it enters a busy-wait loop until it can enter.

5. What is a race condition, and how does Peterson's Algorithm prevent it?

Answer: A race condition is a situation in which the behaviour of a program depends on the relative timing of events, which can leadto unintended results. Peterson's Algorithm prevents race conditions by carefully coordinating the use of flag and turn to ensure that only one process can enter the critical section at a time.

6. Can Peterson's Algorithm handle more than two processes? Why or why not?

Answer: Peterson's Algorithm is designed specifically for two processes. Extending it to handle more processes would require significantmodification, making it less practical for such scenarios.

7. What are the drawbacks or limitations of Peterson's Algorithm?

Answer: Some limitations of Peterson's Algorithm include its suitability for only two processes, its reliance on busy-waiting, and its potentialfor deadlock if not used correctly.

8. How does Peterson's Algorithm handle process priority, if at all?

Answer: Peterson's Algorithm does not inherently handle process priority. It simply provides mutual exclusion for two processes. If process priority needs to be considered, additional mechanisms or algorithms may need to be integrated with Peterson's Algorithm.

9. Can Peterson's Algorithm be implemented in a multi-threaded environment?

Answer: Yes, Peterson's Algorithm can be adapted for use in multi-threaded environments where thread synchronization is required. However, it wouldstill be limited to scenarios involving two threads.

10. In what real-world scenarios might Peterson's Algorithm be used effectively?

Answer: Peterson's Algorithm can be useful in scenarios where two processes or threads need to access a shared resource or critical section, ensuring that only one of them can do so at any given time. This can apply to tasks like resource allocation in operating systems, controlling access to hardware devices, or managing access to shared data structures.

Semaphores

1. What is a semaphore in the context of process synchronization?

Answer: A semaphore is a synchronization construct that is used to control access to shared resources and coordinate the execution of processes in a multi-threaded or multi-process environment.

2. Explain the two main types of semaphores: binary semaphore and counting semaphore.

Answer: A binary semaphore can only have two values, typically 0 and 1, and is often used for mutual exclusion. A counting semaphore can have a range of non-negative integer values and is used to control access to multiple instances of a resource.

3. What are the two fundamental operations associated with semaphores?

Answer: Semaphores support two primary operations: wait (P) and signal (V). The wait operation decreases the semaphore count and blocks if the count is zero. The signal operation increases the semaphore count.

4. How can semaphores be used to provide mutual exclusion among processes or threads?

Answer: A binary semaphore can be used to provide mutual exclusion by ensuring that only one process or thread can enter a critical section at a time. Processes or threads use wait to request access to the critical section and signal to release it.

5. What is a deadlock, and how can semaphores be involved in deadlock situations?

Answer: A deadlock occurs when two or more processes or threads are unable to proceed because they are waiting for resources held by each other. Semaphores can be involved in deadlock if not properly used, for example, if there's a circular dependency in wait operations among processes.

6. Explain the concept of a mutex and how it relates to semaphores.

Answer: A mutex (short for mutual exclusion) is a type of synchronization mechanism often implemented using binary semaphores. It provides mutual exclusion by allowing only one thread or process to access a critical section at a time.

7. What is a reader-writer semaphore, and how does it differ from a regular semaphore?

Answer: A reader-writer semaphore is used to control access to shared resources in scenarios where multiple readers can access simultaneously, but only one writer is allowed. It differs from a regular semaphore by providing different operations and rules for readers and writers.

8. How does a semaphore help in handling producer-consumer problems?

Answer: Semaphores can be used to control access to a shared buffer in a producer-consumer problem. Producers wait when the buffer is full, and consumers wait when the buffer is empty. This ensures that producers and consumers do not access the buffer simultaneously.

9. What is a condition variable, and how does it complement the functionality of semaphores?

Answer: A condition variable is a synchronization primitive that allows threads or processes to wait for a specific condition to be met before proceeding. It complements semaphores by allowing more fine-grained control over synchronization in complex scenarios.

10. Explain how semaphores can be used to implement synchronization barriers among multiple processes or threads.

Answer: Semaphores can be used to implement synchronization barriers by having each process or thread perform a wait operation when it reaches the barrier and a signal operation when it passes the barrier. The barrier ensures that all processes or threads synchronize at a specific point in the program before proceeding.

ONLINE RESOURCES

Practice Paper Link : https://forms.gle/CsoeVYY5ue3oifWs8

QR Code:

Video Link: https://www.youtube.com/playlist?list=PLzlh_31VWEFpIj9tSbhkG9PHg2ZEG26NQ

QR Code:

Chapter 4: Memory Management

Memory Hierarchy

1. What is the memory hierarchy, and why is it important in computer systems?

Answer: The memory hierarchy is a structure of storage devices with varying speeds, capacities, and costs. It is crucial in computer systems because it allows for efficient data access by storing frequently used data in faster, but smaller, memory types and less frequently used data in larger, slower memory types.

2. Describe the typical levels of the memory hierarchy.

Answer: The memory hierarchy typically includes registers, cache memory (L1, L2, L3), main memory (RAM), secondary storage (e.g., hard drives or SSDs), and tertiary storage (e.g., optical disks or tape drives).

3. What is the role of CPU registers in the memory hierarchy, and how do they differ from other memory types?

Answer: CPU registers are the fastest and smallest storage in the hierarchy, located directly within the CPU. They are used for holding data and instructions during the execution of programs. Registers are significantly faster than other memory types, but they have very limited capacity.

4. Explain the concept of cache memory in the memory hierarchy.

Answer: Cache memory is a small, high-speed memory located between the CPU and the main memory. It stores frequently accessed data and instructions to reduce the latency of data retrieval for the CPU.

5. What are the different cache levels (L1, L2, L3), and how do they work together?

Answer: L1 (Level 1) cache is the smallest and fastest, located closest to the CPU core. L2 (Level 2) cache is larger and slower but still faster than main memory. L3 (Level 3) cache, when available, is even larger and slower. They work together to reduce data access times, with L1 being the first line of defense, followed by L2 and, if present, L3.

6. Why is the concept of "hit" and "miss" important in cache memory?

Answer: A "hit" occurs when the data being accessed is found in the cache, resulting in a faster data retrieval. A "miss" occurs when the data is not in the cache and must be retrieved from a slower level of memory, incurring a latency penalty. Tracking hits and misses helps assess cache efficiency.

7. What is the principle of spatial and temporal locality, and how does it influence cache performance?

Answer: Spatial locality refers to accessing data located near recently accessed data, while temporal locality involves repeatedly accessing the same data. Both principles lead to better cache performance, as cache algorithms take advantage of these behaviours to store and retrieve data efficiently.

8. How does virtual memory fit into the memory hierarchy, and what is its role in computer systems?

Answer: Virtual memory extends the main memory by using secondary storage as an extension. It provides the illusion of a large, contiguous memory space for applications, allowing them to execute even when physical RAM is limited. Virtual memory is an integral part of modern computer systems.

9. Explain the trade-offs between memory hierarchy levels in terms of speed, capacity, and cost.

Answer: As you move down the hierarchy, memory becomes slower, larger, and less expensive per byte. The trade-offs involve finding the right balance between speed and capacity while keeping costs manageable.

10. What are the implications of the memory hierarchy for programming and software design?

Answer: Programmers need to consider the hierarchy when optimizing software for performance. This may involve optimizing data structures and access patterns to maximize cache utilization, minimizing the number of memory accesses, and efficiently managing virtual memory resources.

Main Memory

1. What is main memory (RAM), and what is its primary role in a computer system?

Answer: Main memory, or RAM (Random Access Memory), is a volatile, temporary storage component in a computer. Its primary role is to store data and instructions that the CPU actively uses during program execution.

2. Explain the difference between RAM and ROM.

Answer: RAM (Random Access Memory) is volatile memory that stores data and instructions temporarily, and its contents can be read and written. ROM (Read-Only Memory) is non-volatile memory that stores permanent data or firmware, and its contents are typically read-only.

3. What are the two main types of RAM, and how do they differ?

Answer: The two main types of RAM are DRAM (Dynamic RAM) and SRAM (Static RAM). DRAM is slower and less expensive, while SRAM is faster and more costly. SRAM does not require constant refreshing, unlike DRAM.

4. What is the significance of the term "random access" in RAM?

Answer: "Random access" means that data can be read or written to any memory location with the same access time, regardless of the location's physical location. This provides fast and efficient data retrieval.

5. Explain the concept of memory hierarchy and how RAM fits into it.

Answer: The memory hierarchy is a layered structure that includes various memory types with varying speeds and capacities. RAM, being the primary working memory of a computer, is faster than secondary storage but smaller in capacity than storage devices like hard drives or SSDs.

6. What is the distinction between volatile and non-volatile memory, and why is this differentiation important for RAM?

Answer: Volatile memory, like RAM, loses its data when the power is turned off, whereas non-volatile memory retains data even when the power is off. This differentiation is important for RAM because it's designed for fast, temporary data storage.

7. What is a memory cell in RAM, and how is data stored within it?

Answer: A memory cell in RAM is the smallest unit of storage. Data is stored as electrical charges in capacitors within each cell. A charged capacitor represents a binary "1," while a discharged capacitor represents "0."

8. What is the role of a memory controller in managing RAM, and how does it interact with the CPU?

Answer: A memory controller is responsible for coordinating data transfers between the RAM and the CPU. It manages memory requests, data storage, and retrieval, ensuring the CPU can efficiently access and update data in RAM.

9. What is the significance of RAM's clock speed or memory frequency, and how does it affect a computer's performance?

Answer: RAM's clock speed, or memory frequency, determines how quickly data can be read from or written to RAM. Higher clock speeds can lead to improved system performance, particularly in memory-intensive tasks.

10. How does virtual memory relate to physical RAM, and why is it used in modern computer systems?

Answer: Virtual memory uses a portion of secondary storage, such as a hard drive, to extend the effective size of physical RAM. It provides a larger, contiguous addressable space for applications and helps manage memory resources efficiently, especially when physical RAM is limited.

Virtual Memory

1. What is virtual memory, and why is it used in computer systems?

Answer: Virtual memory is a memory management technique that uses a combination of physical RAM and secondary storage (like a hard drive) to provide the illusion of a larger, contiguous addressable memory space. It's used to enable efficient multitasking, extend available memory, and isolate processes.

2. Explain the concept of address translation in virtual memory.

Answer: Address translation is the process of mapping virtual addresses used by programs to physical memory addresses. The translation is managed by the memory management unit (MMU) and is crucial for accessing data stored in physical RAM or secondary storage.

3. What is the role of the page table in virtual memory, and how does it work?

Answer: The page table is a data structure that keeps track of the mapping between virtual addresses and physical memory locations. When a program references a virtual address, the page table is consulted to find the corresponding physical address.

4. How does demand paging contribute to the efficiency of virtual memory systems?

Answer: Demand paging is a strategy where pages of data are loaded into physical memory only when they are needed. This reduces the need for all data to be loaded into RAM at once, saving memory space and improving system efficiency.

5. What is a page fault in the context of virtual memory, and how is it resolved?

Answer: A page fault occurs when a program tries to access a page that is not currently in physical memory. The operating system resolves this by loading the required page from secondary storage into RAM, possibly swapping out another page if necessary.

6. Explain the concept of thrashing in virtual memory systems.

Answer: Thrashing occurs when the system spends a significant portion of its time swapping pages in and out of physical memory due to excessive page faults. This can severely degrade system performance.

7. How does the use of virtual memory impact the memory hierarchy and the concept of locality?

Answer: Virtual memory extends the effective size of physical RAM by using secondary storage. It still adheres to the principles of locality, including spatial and temporal locality, to optimize memory access patterns.

8. What is the significance of the page size (or frame size) in virtual memory systems?

Answer: Page size determines the unit of data that is transferred between secondary storage and physical memory. Smaller page sizes can lead to more efficient memory usage but can also result in a higher overhead due to more frequent page transfers.

9. How does virtual memory affect the management of memory resources and the execution of multiple processes?

Answer: Virtual memory allows multiple processes to run concurrently, as each process can work with its own virtual address space. The operating system manages memory resources, ensuring that processes do not interfere with each other.

10. What are the trade-offs in using virtual memory, and what factors can impact its performance?

Answer: The trade-offs include a performance cost due to the overhead of address translation and page swapping. Factors impacting performance include the size of physical memory, the page size, the efficiency of the page replacement algorithm, and the I/O speed of secondary storage.

Memory Allocation Strategies

1. What is memory allocation in the context of operating systems, and why is it important?

Answer: Memory allocation refers to the process of reserving and assigning portions of the memory to processes. It's essential for efficient resource utilization, preventing memory fragmentation, and ensuring that processes have the memory they need to execute.

2. Explain the difference between static and dynamic memory allocation.

Answer: Static memory allocation assigns memory to a process at compile time, while dynamic memory allocation reserves memory during runtime. Static allocation is fixed and can't change, while dynamic allocation allows for flexibility.

3. What is the role of a memory manager in an operating system, and how does it relate to memory allocation strategies?

Answer: A memory manager is responsible for managing memory allocation and ensuring efficient utilization. It chooses allocation strategies and decides when to allocate and deallocate memory for processes.

4. What is the first-fit memory allocation strategy, and how does it work?

Answer: First-fit allocates the first available block of memory that is large enough to accommodate a process. It's a simple and fast strategy but can lead to memory fragmentation over time.

5. Describe the best-fit memory allocation strategy and its advantages and disadvantages.

Answer: Best-fit allocates the smallest available block of memory that can accommodate a process. It minimizes fragmentation but can lead to inefficient use of memory due to small, unused gaps.

6. What is the worst-fit memory allocation strategy, and why is it rarely used in practice?

Answer: Worst-fit allocates the largest available block of memory for a process. This strategy is rarely used because it leads to extensive memory fragmentation and may not be efficient in practice.

7. Explain the buddy memory allocation method and its application in memory allocation.

Answer: Buddy allocation divides memory into blocks that are powers of 2 in size and allocates memory based on these block sizes. It's often used in systems that manage memory as a binary tree structure to minimize fragmentation.

8. What is memory compaction, and why is it useful in memory allocation strategies?

Answer: Memory compaction is the process of rearranging memory to eliminate fragmentation. It helps in maximizing the available free memory for allocation, thus reducing the chances of allocation failures.

9. Describe the concept of paging in memory allocation and how it works.

Answer: Paging divides physical memory and processes' address spaces into fixed-size blocks called pages. It simplifies memory allocation by mapping pages between physical and virtual memory, allowing for efficient memory utilization.

10. How does segmentation differ from paging in memory allocation strategies?

Answer: Segmentation divides memory into segments that correspond to different parts of a program, such as code, data, and stack. Paging, on the other hand, divides memory into fixed-size pages. Segmentation is more flexible but can lead to fragmentation. Paging provides efficient memory utilization but may be less intuitive.

Page Replacement Algorithms

1 What is the role of page replacement algorithms in virtual memory management?

Answer: Page replacement algorithms determine which page in physical memory should be replaced when a page fault occurs, ensuring that the most relevant pages are retained in memory.

2. Explain the FIFO (First-In, First-Out) page replacement algorithm. How does it work, and what are its drawbacks?

Answer: FIFO replaces the oldest page in memory with the new incoming page. It's simple to implement but suffers from the "Belady's Anomaly," where increasing the number of frames may lead to more page faults.

3. What is the LRU (Least Recently Used) page replacement algorithm, and how does it prioritize pages for replacement?

Answer: LRU replaces the page that has not been used for the longest time. It prioritizes pages based on their historical access patterns. LRU is effective but can be challenging to implement efficiently.

4. Describe the Second-Chance (Clock) page replacement algorithm and how it mitigates the issue of LRU implementation complexity.

Answer: Second-Chance is a variation of LRU that uses a circular list. It gives pages a "second chance" before replacing them. If a page is referenced, it is moved to the end of the list, providing a simple approximation of LRU without the need to track precise usage timestamps.

5. What is the Optimal (MIN) page replacement algorithm, and why is it considered the "ideal" algorithm?

Answer: The Optimal algorithm replaces the page that will not be used for the longest time in the future. It is considered ideal because it minimizes the number of page faults. However, it is not practically implementable because it requires knowledge of future page accesses.

6. Explain the advantages and disadvantages of the LRU approximation algorithm using counters.

Answer: The LRU approximation algorithm using counters assigns a counter to each page and increments it when the page is accessed. It approximates LRU and is easier to implement than actual LRU. However, it requires additional memory to store counters, which can be a drawback.

What is the difference between the LFU (Least Frequently Used) and MFU (Most Frequently Used) page replacement algorithms?

Answer: LFU replaces the page that has been used the least number of times, while MFU replaces the page that has been used the most frequently. Both algorithms prioritize pages based on usage frequency.

Explain the concept of the Working Set page replacement algorithm and how it helps in reducing page faults.

Answer: The Working Set algorithm maintains a "working set" of pages for each process, tracking the pages accessed within a fixed time window. By ensuring that pages in the working set remain in memory, it reduces page faults for active processes.

What is the concept of the WSClock page replacement algorithm, and how does it combine elements of both LRU and Second-Chance algorithms?

Answer: WSClock is a page replacement algorithm that maintains a circular list of pages with additional reference and modify bits. It combines aspects of both LRU and Second-Chance by using the reference and modify bits to decide which pages to replace, prioritizing modified pages over unmodified ones.

How do global and local page replacement algorithms differ, and when might one be preferred over the other?

Answer: Global algorithms consider the entire system when making page replacement decisions, whereas local algorithms consider only the pages of a single process. Global algorithms can be fairer among processes but are more complex to implement, while local algorithms are simpler but may not make the best overall system decisions. The choice depends on the specific requirements and goals of the system.

ONLINE RESOURCES

Practice Paper Link : https://forms.gle/ko5f7AwoMRwZqtQV8

QR Code :

Video Link: https://www.youtube.com/playlist?list=PLzlh_31VWEFr0nhNKvQouAwg1OdvsTSMu

QR Code :

Chapter 5: File Systems

File Concept

1. What is a file in the context of an operating system?

Answer: In an operating system, a file is a logical unit of data storage that can represent various types of information, such as text, images, programs, or documents. Files provide a structured way to store, access, and organize data.

2. What are the key attributes associated with a file, and how are they used in file management?

Answer: The key attributes of a file include its name, size, type, location, creation/modification timestamps, and permissions. These attributes are used for identification, access control, and tracking changes in files.

3. Explain the difference between a file and a directory.

Answer: A file is a container for data, while a directory is a container for files and other directories. Files contain information, while directories provide a hierarchical structure for organizing and managing files.

4. What is the purpose of a file extension, and how does it relate to file types?

Answer: A file extension is a suffix in a file name that indicates the file type or format. It helps both users and the operating system identify the nature of the file and the appropriate application to use when opening it.

5. What is the role of the file system in managing files, and how does it organize data on storage devices?

Answer: The file system is responsible for organizing and managing files on storage devices. It uses data structures, such as directories, to create a logical structure for files, making them easy to locate and access.

6. Explain the concept of file access permissions and how they ensure data security in an operating system.

Answer: File access permissions define who can read, write, or execute a file. They help ensure data security by restricting access to authorized users and preventing unauthorized access or modifications.

7. What are the common file operations supported by operating systems, such as read, write, open, close, and delete?

Answer: Common file operations include opening a file for reading or writing, closing a file after use, reading data from a file, writing data to a file, and deleting files when they are no longer needed.

8. What is a file path, and how does it help locate files in a file system?

Answer: A file path is a textual representation of the file's location within the file system's directory structure. It includes the directory names and file name, allowing the operating system to locate the file.

9. Describe the difference between a relative path and an absolute path in file navigation.

Answer: A relative path is specified relative to the current working directory, while an absolute path specifies the full directory path from the root directory. Absolute paths provide the exact location, while relative paths depend on the current context.

10. What is file fragmentation, and how can it affect file system performance?

Answer: File fragmentation occurs when a file is stored in non-contiguous blocks on a storage device. It can lead to slower file access times because the storage device's read/write head must move between different locations on the disk, increasing seek times. File defragmentation tools can be used to optimize file placement and improve performance.

File Operations

1. What are file operations in an operating system, and why are they important?

Answer: File operations refer to the tasks that can be performed on files, including creation, reading, writing, updating, and deletion. They are vital for managing data and resources in a computer system.

2. Explain the fundamental file operations: open, read, write, close, and delete.

Answer:

Open: It initiates access to a file and provides a file descriptor.

Read: It retrieves data from a file into a buffer.

Write: It stores data from a buffer into a file.

Close: It terminates file access, releasing associated resources.

Delete: It removes a file from the file system.

3. What is the purpose of the open system call in file operations?

Answer: The open system call is used to initiate access to a file. It allocates necessary resources, sets up a file descriptor for subsequent operations, and returns a unique identifier for the file.

4. Explain how file permissions are used to control access in file operations.

Answer: File permissions specify which users or groups can perform specific operations on a file. They include read, write, and execute permissions, which determine who can view, modify, or run a file, respectively.

5. What is the role of buffering in file operations, and how does it impact I/O performance?

Answer: Buffering involves temporarily storing data in memory before reading from or writing to a file. It can enhance I/O performance by reducing the number of actual disk accesses, as data can be transferred in larger, more efficient chunks.

6. How does file locking work in file operations, and what is its significance in multi-process environments?

Answer: File locking prevents multiple processes from concurrently accessing or modifying a file. It ensures data integrity and prevents race conditions in multi-process environments by allowing exclusive access to a file when necessary.

7. Explain the difference between synchronous and asynchronous I/O operations in file handling.

Answer: Synchronous I/O operations block the process until the I/O operation is complete, while asynchronous I/O allows the process to continue execution while the operation is in progress. Asynchronous I/O can improve overall system responsiveness.

8. What is file versioning, and how can it be implemented in file operations?

Answer: File versioning involves maintaining multiple versions of a file to track changes over time. It can be implemented by creating backups or using revision control systems like Git to manage file versions.

9. What are the potential challenges when performing file operations on networked file systems compared to local file systems?

Answer: Challenges with networked file systems may include latency, data consistency, and security issues. Networked file systems require data to be transferred over a network, which can introduce delays, and maintaining data consistency among multiple users or systems can be more complex.

10. What are symbolic links in file operations, and how do they differ from hard links?

Answer: Symbolic links are references to other files or directories, while hard links are multiple directory entries pointing to the same inode. Symbolic links are distinct files and can span across file systems, while hard links share the same inode and must reside on the same file system.

File System Structure

1. What is the file system structure in an operating system, and why is it essential?

Answer: The file system structure is the organization and layout of files and directories on storage devices. It's essential for efficient data storage, retrieval, and management in an operating system.

2. Explain the concept of a directory in a file system and its role in organizing files.

Answer: A directory is a logical container for organizing and categorizing files. It provides a hierarchical structure, allowing files to be grouped, named, and accessed more conveniently.

3. What is a file path, and how is it used in the file system structure to locate files?

Answer: A file path is a textual representation of a file's location within the directory structure. It includes directory names and file names, guiding the operating system to find and access files.

4. Describe the difference between an absolute path and a relative path in the context of file system navigation.

Answer: An absolute path specifies the complete directory hierarchy from the root directory, while a relative path is specified relative to the current working directory. Absolute paths provide an exact location, while relative paths depend on the current context.

5. Explain the significance of the root directory in the file system structure.

Answer: The root directory is the top-level directory in the file system hierarchy. All other directories and files are organized beneath it. It serves as the starting point for file system navigation.

6. What is a file descriptor, and how does it relate to the file system structure?

Answer: A file descriptor is an identifier used by the operating system to represent an open file. It points to the file's location within the file system structure and contains information needed for I/O operations.

7. What are the advantages of a tree-like directory structure, and how does it compare to a flat directory structure?

Answer: A tree-like directory structure offers a hierarchical organization that allows for better file organization and management. It simplifies file access and avoids naming conflicts, compared to a flat structure where all files are stored in a single directory.

8. Explain the concept of a file path separator and its use in different operating systems (e.g., '/' in Unix/Linux, '' in Windows).

Answer: A file path separator is a character used to separate directory and file names in a path. In Unix/Linux, the forward slash (/) is used, while in Windows, the backslash () is used. Understanding the appropriate separator is essential for cross-platform compatibility.

9. What are inodes, and how do they relate to the file system structure in Unix-based operating systems?

Answer: Inodes are data structures in Unix-based file systems that store metadata about files and directories, including file permissions, ownership, size, and pointers to data blocks. They are crucial for locating and managing files within the file system structure.

10. How does the file system structure impact data retrieval and storage efficiency in an operating system?

Answer: A well-organized file system structure improves data retrieval and storage efficiency by facilitating quick and efficient file access, reducing the risk of naming conflicts, and enabling effective data management.

File System Implementation

1. What is file system implementation in the context of an operating system, and why is it important?

Answer: File system implementation refers to the actual mechanisms and algorithms used to manage files and directories on storage devices. It is crucial for efficient and reliable storage, retrieval, and management of data.

2. Explain the role of the file system implementation in managing file metadata.

Answer: File system implementation manages file metadata, including file attributes (e.g., name, size, permissions), and keeps track of data block locations on the storage device. This information is essential for file access and management.

3. How do file system implementation choices impact storage efficiency and performance in an operating system?

Answer: File system implementation choices, such as data structures and algorithms, can significantly impact storage efficiency and performance. Efficient data structures and algorithms reduce access times, optimize storage space, and improve overall system performance.

4. What is a file allocation table (FAT), and how is it used in file system implementation?

Answer: A file allocation table (FAT) is a data structure used in some file systems to track the allocation status of data blocks on storage devices. It helps manage file storage, determine free space, and locate file data blocks.

5. Describe the concept of block-based file systems and their use in file system implementation.

Answer: Block-based file systems store data in fixed-size blocks, making data allocation and management more efficient. They are commonly used in file system implementations due to their simplicity and predictability.

6. What are journaling file systems, and how do they improve data consistency in the event of system crashes or failures?

Answer: Journaling file systems maintain a journal that logs changes before they are applied to the file system. In the event of a crash, the journal helps restore data consistency by replaying or undoing transactions.

7. Explain the advantages and disadvantages of file system fragmentation, and how it is managed in file system implementation.

Answer: File system fragmentation can lead to inefficient space utilization and slower file access. File system implementations use strategies like defragmentation to reduce fragmentation and improve performance.

8. What is a file system superblock, and how does it contribute to the integrity and reliability of the file system?

Answer: A file system superblock is a critical data structure that contains essential information about the file system. It helps ensure the file system's integrity by maintaining metadata, such as the file system size, block sizes, and free space tracking.

9. How do file system implementations handle concurrent access to files by multiple processes, and why is this important?

Answer: File system implementations use locking mechanisms and access control to manage concurrent access to files. This is crucial to prevent data corruption, maintain data integrity, and provide secure access in multi-user environments.

10. Explain the role of the file system cache in file system implementation and how it impacts I/O performance.

Answer: The file system cache stores frequently accessed data in memory to reduce the need for reading and writing to storage devices. It significantly improves I/O performance by reducing latency and minimizing actual disk accesses.

Directory and Disk Structure

1. What is the role of a directory in an operating system, and why is it important?

Answer: A directory is a logical container for organizing and managing files. It provides a hierarchical structure for efficient data organization, storage, and retrieval.

2. Explain the concept of a directory tree in the context of an operating system and how it is used for file management.

Answer: A directory tree is a hierarchical structure formed by nesting directories within other directories. It allows for systematic organization of files and subdirectories, making it easier to locate and manage data.

3. What is the root directory in a file system, and why is it significant?

Answer: The root directory is the top-level directory in a file system. It is significant because it serves as the starting point for the entire directory hierarchy and contains references to all other directories and files.

4. How do file paths help in navigating the directory structure, and what is the difference between absolute and relative file paths?

Answer: File paths are textual representations that guide the operating system to locate and access files or directories within the directory structure. An absolute file path specifies the full path from the root directory, while a relative file path is specified relative to the current working directory.

5. What is a mount point, and how does it relate to the directory structure on different storage devices in an operating system?

Answer: A mount point is a directory in a file system where another file system is attached or "mounted." It links directories on different storage devices, allowing access to files and directories on secondary devices as if they were part of the primary file system.

6. Explain the concept of a directory entry and how it relates to the directory structure.

Answer: A directory entry is a data structure associated with a file or subdirectory. It contains metadata about the file, such as the name and location, allowing the operating system to manage and access the file within the directory structure.

7. What is a file allocation table (FAT), and how is it used in directory and disk structure?

Answer: A file allocation table (FAT) is a data structure used in some file systems to keep track of data block allocations on storage devices. It helps manage file storage, locate data blocks, and organize the directory structure.

8. How does the directory structure impact storage device management, and what is the role of the file system in this context?

Answer: The directory structure impacts storage device management by providing a logical organization for files and directories. The file system ensures proper data storage, retrieval, and management by organizing data on the storage device.

9. What is the purpose of directory links (or symbolic links), and how do they affect the directory structure?

Answer: Directory links, or symbolic links, are references to other directories or files. They allow for the creation of shortcuts to access files or directories in different locations within the directory structure.

10. Explain the difference between a file system's logical structure and its physical structure, and how they interact to manage data.

Answer: The logical structure of a file system refers to the hierarchical organization of directories and files. The physical structure involves the actual layout of data on the storage device. The logical structure helps users and applications navigate the file system, while the physical structure determines data storage efficiency and access times. Both structures work together to manage data effectively.

File Security and Permissions

1. What is the significance of file security and permissions in an operating system?

Answer: File security and permissions control who can access, modify, or execute files, ensuring data integrity, confidentiality, and system security.

2. Explain the three basic file permissions: read, write, and execute.

Answer:

Read: Allows a user to view the contents of a file.

Write: Permits a user to modify or delete the file.

Execute: Grants permission to run an executable file or script.

3. What are the three user categories typically associated with file permissions, and how do they differ?

Answer: The three user categories are:

Owner: The user who owns the file and can set its permissions.

Group: A group of users who share the same permissions.

Others: All users who are not the owner or in the group.

4. Explain the difference between file permissions for the owner, group, and others.

Answer:

The owner can set read, write, and execute permissions.

The group can have separate read, write, and execute permissions.

Others can also have distinct read, write, and execute permissions.

5. What is the purpose of the "umask" value in file security, and how does it influence default file permissions?

Answer: The "umask" value is a permission mask that subtracts from the maximum file permissions when a new file is created. It influences default file permissions by specifying which permissions are removed.

6. Explain the concept of the "execute" permission for directories and its significance.

Answer: The "execute" permission on directories allows users to navigate (cd) into the directory. Without it, users cannot access or list the contents of the directory. This permission is crucial for directory traversal.

7. What are the symbolic and octal representations of file permissions, and how are they used to set and modify permissions?

Answer:

Symbolic representation (e.g., "rwxr-xr--") uses letters (r, w, x) for read, write, and execute, while octal representation (e.g., 755) uses numerical values to represent permissions. These representations are used with commands like "chmod" to set or modify permissions.

8. What is the concept of "chmod" in file security, and how is it used to change file permissions?

Answer: "chmod" is a command used to change file permissions. It can add or remove specific permissions for the owner, group, and others using either symbolic or octal notation.

9. What is the "chown" command, and how does it relate to file security and ownership?

Answer: The "chown" command is used to change the ownership of a file. It is essential for file security, as it allows administrators to transfer ownership to other users or groups.

10. Explain the concept of "suid," "sgid," and "sticky" bits in file permissions, and their use cases.

Answer:

SUID (Set User ID): When set on an executable file, it runs with the permissions of the file owner. Useful for allowing users to run certain programs with elevated privileges.

SGID (Set Group ID): When set on an executable file, it runs with the permissions of the file's group. Useful for maintaining a specific group's permissions when multiple users access a file.

Sticky Bit: When set on a directory, it restricts file deletion to the file owner. Typically used on directories where multiple users have write access, like /tmp.

ONLINE RESOURCES

Practice Paper Link : https://forms.gle/k6y748T6tJae7mZ46

QR Code:

Video Link: https://www.youtube.com/playlist?list=PLzlh_31VWEFpYotpexo0YDwU1qUtbFYUv

QR Code:

Chapter 6: I/O Systems

I/O Hardware

1. What is I/O hardware in the context of operating systems, and why is it important?

Answer: I/O hardware includes devices like keyboards, displays, storage drives, and network interfaces that facilitate data input and output. It is essential for communication between the computer and external devices.

2. Explain the distinction between synchronous and asynchronous I/O operations in the context of I/O hardware.

Answer: Synchronous I/O operations block the calling process until the operation is complete, while asynchronous I/O allows the process to continue execution while the operation is in progress, improving overall system responsiveness.

3. How do device drivers relate to I/O hardware, and what is their role in an operating system?

Answer: Device drivers are software components that enable communication between the operating system and hardware devices. They provide a standardized interface for the OS to interact with various hardware components.

4. What is the purpose of I/O ports and memory-mapped I/O in connecting I/O devices to the CPU, and how do they differ?

Answer: I/O ports and memory-mapped I/O are methods for the CPU to communicate with I/O devices. I/O ports use separate address space for devices, while memory-mapped I/O allocates device registers within the main memory address space.

5. Explain the concept of polling and interrupt-driven I/O mechanisms and their impact on CPU utilization.

Answer: Polling involves the CPU periodically checking the status of an I/O device, which can lead to high CPU utilization. Interrupt-driven I/O allows devices to notify the CPU when they are ready for data transfer, reducing CPU usage.

6. What is Direct Memory Access (DMA), and how does it improve I/O efficiency in the presence of high-speed devices?

Answer: DMA allows devices to directly access system memory for data transfer, bypassing the CPU. It enhances I/O efficiency by reducing CPU involvement and enabling faster data transfer with high-speed devices.

7. Explain the concept of I/O buffering and how it optimizes data transfer between devices and memory.

Answer: I/O buffering involves temporarily storing data in memory buffers before transferring it between devices and memory. It optimizes data transfer by allowing efficient block I/O, reducing the frequency of small, individual transfers.

8. What is I/O scheduling in the context of storage devices, and why is it important for disk performance?

Answer: I/O scheduling refers to the order in which pending I/O requests are serviced. It is essential for disk performance because it can minimize seek times and improve overall I/O efficiency.

9. Explain the concept of hot swapping in I/O hardware and its significance for system maintenance.

Answer: Hot swapping allows I/O devices to be replaced or added while the system is running. This is significant for minimizing system downtime during maintenance or when upgrading hardware.

10. What are I/O control registers, and how do they facilitate communication between the CPU and I/O devices?

Answer: I/O control registers are special hardware registers that allow the CPU to send commands and receive status information from I/O devices. They provide a standardized interface for device communication.

Principles of I/O Software

1. What are the fundamental principles of I/O software in operating systems, and why are they important?

Answer: The fundamental principles of I/O software include transparency, efficiency, and uniformity. Transparency hides device-specific details from applications, efficiency maximizes I/O performance, and uniformity provides a consistent interface for diverse devices.

2. Explain the concept of device independence in I/O software and how it benefits the operating system.

Answer: Device independence allows applications to access I/O devices without needing to know the specifics of each device. It simplifies application development and enhances portability, as the same code can work with different devices.

3. What is the role of device drivers in I/O software, and how do they provide device independence to the operating system?

Answer: Device drivers are software components that interface between the operating system and I/O devices. They provide device independence by abstracting the hardware details, enabling the OS to communicate with various devices in a uniform manner.

4. How does the principle of uniform naming in I/O software simplify device management and resource allocation?

Answer: Uniform naming ensures that devices are referenced consistently across the system, simplifying device management and making it easier for the OS to allocate resources and manage access permissions.

5. Explain the concept of buffering in I/O software and its impact on I/O performance.

Answer: Buffering involves temporarily storing data in memory before transferring it between devices and applications. It improves I/O performance by reducing the overhead of frequent disk or network access and optimizing data transfer sizes.

6. What are the advantages and disadvantages of synchronous and asynchronous I/O operations in I/O software?

Answer: Synchronous I/O operations are simpler but may lead to wasted CPU time, while asynchronous I/O allows processes to continue executing during I/O, improving overall system responsiveness but requiring more complex programming.

7. What is spooling, and how does it ensure efficient device utilization in I/O software?

Answer: Spooling (Simultaneous Peripheral Operation On-Line) allows multiple I/O requests to be queued for devices. It ensures efficient device utilization by minimizing idle times, enabling devices to handle multiple tasks in parallel.

8. Explain the role of I/O scheduling in I/O software and how it impacts disk performance.

Answer: I/O scheduling determines the order in which pending I/O requests are serviced. It can minimize seek times, reduce contention, and improve disk performance by optimizing the order in which requests are processed.

9. What is the purpose of error handling and recovery in I/O software, and how does it contribute to system reliability?

Answer: Error handling and recovery mechanisms in I/O software detect and correct errors during I/O operations, contributing to system reliability by minimizing data loss, system crashes, or data corruption due to I/O errors.

10. How does the concept of I/O virtualization in I/O software impact resource management and isolation in virtualized environments?

Answer: I/O virtualization abstracts physical devices into virtual devices for virtual machines (VMs). It improves resource management and isolation by allowing VMs to access and use virtual devices without conflicts and enabling the efficient sharing of physical resources.

Disk Structure and Management

1. What is the disk structure in an operating system, and why is it important for data storage?

Answer: The disk structure represents the organization of data on storage devices like hard drives. It is essential for efficient data storage, retrieval, and management in an operating system.

2. Explain the concept of a disk block and its role in data storage and management.

Answer: A disk block is the smallest addressable unit on a storage device. It serves as the basic unit for data storage, retrieval, and management. Files are stored in one or more blocks, making it easier to manage and allocate storage space.

3. What are the differences between a disk partition and a file system, and how do they work together?

Answer: A disk partition is a logical section of a storage device, while a file system defines the structure and organization of files within a partition. A disk can have multiple partitions, each with its file system, to manage data.

4. Explain the role of a master boot record (MBR) or GUID Partition Table (GPT) in disk structure and management.

Answer: MBR and GPT are used to store information about partitions on a disk. MBR is the older standard, while GPT is newer and more versatile. They help the operating system locate and manage partitions on a disk.

5. What is a file allocation unit, and how does it affect disk space utilization in file systems?

Answer: A file allocation unit, also known as a cluster or block size, is the minimum unit of disk space allocation. It can impact space utilization because files occupy entire clusters, potentially leading to wasted space for small files.

6. Explain the concept of fragmentation in disk structure and management and how it impacts file system performance.

Answer: Fragmentation occurs when files are stored in non-contiguous blocks on a disk. It can lead to slower access times, as the read/write head needs to move between different locations. Defragmentation tools are used to optimize file placement.

7. What is the role of disk caching in disk management, and how does it impact I/O performance?

Answer: Disk caching involves storing frequently accessed data in memory. It significantly improves I/O performance by reducing the need for reading and writing to the disk and minimizing access times.

8. Explain the purpose of the file system's directory structure in disk management and data organization.

Answer: The directory structure provides a hierarchical organization for files and directories. It simplifies file organization, makes data more accessible, and helps users locate and manage files efficiently.

9. How does the concept of bad blocks or bad sectors impact disk management, and how are they handled in file systems?

Answer: Bad blocks are damaged or unreliable portions of a disk. They can affect data integrity and system performance. File systems often include mechanisms to mark bad blocks and avoid using them to ensure data reliability.

10. What is the purpose of disk quotas in disk management, and how do they help in controlling disk space usage?

Answer: Disk quotas are used to limit the amount of disk space that users or groups can consume. They help in controlling disk space usage, preventing one user from monopolizing the disk and ensuring fair allocation of resources.

Disk Scheduling Algorithms

1. What is the purpose of disk scheduling algorithms in operating systems?

Answer: Disk scheduling algorithms determine the order in which I/O requests are serviced to minimize seek time and improve disk access performance.

2. Explain the FCFS (First-Come, First-Served) disk scheduling algorithm.

Answer: FCFS schedules I/O requests in the order they arrive. The first request in the queue is the first to be serviced.

3. What is the main drawback of the FCFS disk scheduling algorithm, and how does it affect disk performance?

Answer: The main drawback of FCFS is the lack of optimization based on the physical location of data. This can result in poor performance due to the "seek time" problem.

4. How does the SSTF (Shortest Seek Time First) disk scheduling algorithm work, and what advantage does it offer over FCFS?

Answer: SSTF schedules I/O requests based on the closest available track to the current head position. It minimizes seek time by selecting the nearest request, offering better performance than FCFS.

5. What is the major disadvantage of SSTF, and how does it impact certain requests?

Answer: The disadvantage of SSTF is that it may lead to the starvation of requests located far from the head, as it prioritizes the nearest requests.

6. Explain the SCAN (Elevator Algorithm) disk scheduling algorithm.

Answer: SCAN schedules I/O requests by moving the disk arm from one end of the disk to the other, servicing requests along the way. It reverses direction when it reaches the end.

7. How does the LOOK disk scheduling algorithm differ from SCAN, and what advantage does it provide?

Answer: LOOK is similar to SCAN but changes direction when there are no pending requests in the current direction. It reduces seek time and minimizes delays for nearby requests.

8. What is the primary advantage of the C-LOOK (Circular LOOK) disk scheduling algorithm over C-SCAN?

Answer: C-LOOK restricts head movement to one direction, like C-SCAN, but it eliminates some of the delays found in C-SCAN by not servicing the entire disk.

9. What is the N-Step-SCAN (N-Step-Look) disk scheduling algorithm, and in what scenarios is it particularly useful?

Answer: N-Step-SCAN services multiple requests at a time, reducing the overhead of repositioning the disk arm. It is efficient for batch processing scenarios, where multiple contiguous requests can be serviced together.

10. How does the choice of a disk scheduling algorithm depend on the specific use case and system priorities?

Answer: The choice of a disk scheduling algorithm depends on factors such as the system's I/O workload, the need for low latency, and the desire for fairness in servicing requests. Different algorithms are suitable for various use cases and priorities.

I/O Device Handling

1. What is I/O device handling, and why is it a critical aspect of an operating system?

Answer: I/O device handling involves managing the communication and interaction between the operating system and various I/O devices. It's essential for ensuring data transfer, device synchronization, and resource management in a computer system.

2. Explain the role of device drivers in I/O device handling.

Answer: Device drivers are software components that act as intermediaries between the operating system and hardware devices. They provide a standardized interface for the OS to communicate with specific devices, translating OS requests into device-specific commands.

3. What are the challenges of managing multiple I/O devices concurrently in an operating system, and how are these challenges addressed?

Answer: Challenges include device contention, prioritization, and ensuring fairness. These are addressed by using various scheduling algorithms, interrupt-driven mechanisms, and resource allocation policies.

4. Describe the process of device initialization and configuration in I/O device handling.

Answer: Device initialization involves setting up hardware devices for proper operation. Configuration typically includes loading device drivers, setting device parameters, and ensuring device compatibility with the system.

5. What is the purpose of interrupt handling in I/O device management, and how does it improve system responsiveness?

Answer: Interrupt handling allows devices to signal the CPU when they need attention. It improves system responsiveness by enabling asynchronous I/O operations and reducing the CPU's polling overhead.

6. Explain the concept of direct memory access (DMA) and how it affects I/O device handling.

Answer: DMA allows devices to transfer data directly to and from memory without CPU involvement. It enhances I/O device handling by improving data transfer efficiency and reducing CPU load.

7. How does the operating system handle device errors and failures in I/O device management, and what mechanisms are in place for recovery?

Answer: The OS employs error handling mechanisms, which may include error codes, retries, and logging. Some devices provide error correction and recovery mechanisms built into their hardware.

8. What is the role of I/O control registers in device handling, and how do they facilitate communication between the CPU and devices?

Answer: I/O control registers are special hardware registers that provide a standardized interface for the CPU to send commands and receive status information from I/O devices, enhancing device communication.

9. Explain the concept of device spooling and its significance in I/O device handling.

Answer: Spooling (Simultaneous Peripheral Operation On-Line) is a technique that queues I/O requests for devices to improve device utilization and reduce idle time. It helps maintain a steady flow of I/O operations and ensures efficient resource usage.

10. What role does device virtualization play in I/O device handling, and how does it contribute to efficient resource management in virtualized environments?

Answer: Device virtualization abstracts physical devices into virtual devices for virtual machines (VMs). It enhances resource management by allowing VMs to access and use virtual devices without conflicts, enabling efficient sharing of physical resources.

Block and Character Devices

1. What are block and character devices, and how do they differ in the context of I/O in operating systems?

Answer: Block devices are capable of reading and writing data in fixed-size blocks, while character devices process data as a stream of characters without regard to block sizes. Block devices are typically used for file systems and storage devices, while character devices are used for input and output, like keyboards and serial ports.

2. Explain the key characteristics of block devices and provide examples of common block devices.

Answer: Block devices use fixed-size blocks for data transfer, are typically used for storing data, and allow random access. Examples of block devices include hard drives, SSDs, and USB drives.

3. What are the primary characteristics of character devices, and can you provide examples of common character devices?

Answer: Character devices handle data as a stream of characters, are used for input and output, and do not have a fixed block size. Examples of character devices include keyboards, mice, and serial ports.

4. How does the operating system differentiate between block and character devices, and what is the significance of this differentiation?

Answer: The OS identifies devices based on their unique device numbers. The differentiation is crucial because it allows the OS to apply appropriate I/O operations and data transfer methods to each type of device.

5. Explain the concept of buffering and caching in the context of block and character devices.

Answer: Buffers and caches are used for data storage and retrieval in both block and character devices. Buffers store data temporarily before or after an I/O operation, while caches store frequently accessed data to improve performance.

6. How does the concept of seek time apply to block devices, and why is it relevant for their performance?

Answer: Seek time is the time taken for the read/write head to move to the desired data location on block devices. It's crucial for performance, as minimizing seek time reduces latency in data access.

7. Explain the role of the device driver in managing block and character devices.

Answer: Device drivers provide the necessary software interface between the operating system and hardware devices. They manage device-specific details and ensure data transfer and communication.

8. How does the choice between block and character devices affect the performance and functionality of I/O operations in an operating system?

Answer: Block devices are optimized for data storage and random access, while character devices are suitable for handling character-oriented data streams. The choice depends on the specific use case and performance requirements.

What is the significance of block sizes in block devices, and how can it impact data storage efficiency?

Answer: Block sizes determine the granularity of data storage on block devices. Choosing an appropriate block size is crucial for data storage efficiency, as it can impact space utilization and I/O performance.

In the context of block and character devices, how does the operating system handle I/O requests and prioritize them for execution?

Answer: The OS maintains queues of I/O requests for both types of devices. These queues are managed using scheduling algorithms, ensuring fair and efficient execution of I/O operations. Block devices may prioritize read and write requests differently based on factors like data integrity and latency.

ONLINE RESOURCES

Practice Paper Link : https://forms.gle/7yBJfd882NrgLzt7A

QR Code:

VideoLink:https://www.youtube.com/playlist?list=PLzlh_31VWEFq2JYMcMOyDkMIOGQabt8_8

QR Code:

Chapter 7: Distributed Systems

Distributed Operating Systems

1. What is a distributed operating system, and how does it differ from a traditional, single-node operating system?

Answer: A distributed operating system is designed to manage and coordinate the operation of multiple interconnected nodes or computers. It differs from traditional operating systems by extending its functionality to handle networked communication, resource sharing, and distributed application management.

2. What are some key advantages of using a distributed operating system in a networked environment?

Answer: Distributed operating systems offer advantages such as resource sharing, fault tolerance, load balancing, scalability, and improved performance through parallel processing.

3. Explain the concept of transparency in distributed operating systems.

Answer: Transparency in distributed operating systems refers to the ability to hide the complexities of the distributed nature from users and applications. It includes transparency in access, location, migration, concurrency, and failure.

4. What is the role of middleware in a distributed operating system, and how does it facilitate communication and interaction between nodes?

Answer: Middleware is software that sits between the distributed applications and the operating system, providing services like communication protocols, naming, security, and data marshalling. It facilitates inter-node communication and interaction by abstracting low-level details.

5. How does a distributed operating system handle issues related to security and access control in a networked environment?

Answer: Distributed operating systems use authentication, encryption, and access control mechanisms to ensure secure data transfer and enforce access policies across the network.

6. What challenges do distributed operating systems face in terms of consistency and synchronization of data across multiple nodes?

Answer: Maintaining data consistency and synchronization in a distributed environment is challenging due to network latency, node failures, and concurrent access. Distributed systems use techniques like distributed locks, transactions, and version control to address these issues.

7. What is the significance of fault tolerance in distributed operating systems, and how is it achieved?

Answer: Fault tolerance is crucial for ensuring system reliability. It is achieved by redundancy, replication, and mechanisms like leader election and consensus algorithms to handle failures gracefully.

8. Explain the role of load balancing in distributed operating systems and how it improves system performance.

Answer: Load balancing distributes incoming requests and tasks evenly among multiple nodes, ensuring that no single node is overwhelmed. This improves system performance by maximizing resource utilization and minimizing response times.

9. What is the concept of remote procedure calls (RPC) in distributed operating systems, and how do they enable communication between processes on different nodes?

Answer: RPC is a mechanism that allows a process on one node to invoke a procedure on a remote node, making it appear as if the procedure is local. It simplifies distributed application development by abstracting network communication details.

10. How does a distributed operating system handle distributed file systems and provide access to shared files across the network?

Answer: Distributed file systems allow users to access and share files across multiple nodes. The operating system coordinates these activities by managing file access, consistency, caching, and replication to ensure efficient and reliable file sharing.

Networking Fundamentals

1. What is a computer network, and why are they important in the modern world?

Answer: A computer network is a collection of interconnected devices that can share data and resources. Networks are essential for communication, resource sharing, and information exchange, facilitating collaboration and connectivity.

2. Explain the difference between LAN, WAN, and MAN.

Answer:LAN (Local Area Network) is a network that covers a small geographic area, like a single building or campus.

WAN (Wide Area Network) spans larger areas, often across cities or countries.

MAN (Metropolitan Area Network) covers a city or a large campus, bridging the gap between LAN and WAN.

3. What is the OSI model, and why is it important in networking?

Answer: The OSI (Open Systems Interconnection) model is a conceptual framework used to standardize network communication. It's important because it defines seven layers that help in understanding and troubleshooting network protocols and systems.

4. What are the primary functions of the TCP/IP protocol suite, and how does it relate to the OSI model?

Answer: The TCP/IP protocol suite is the foundation of the internet and encompasses protocols like TCP, IP, and others. It provides end-to-end communication and aligns closely with the OSI model, mapping roughly to its layers.

5. Explain the purpose of an IP address and the differences between IPv4 and IPv6.

Answer: An IP address is a unique identifier for devices on a network. IPv4 uses 32-bit addresses, while IPv6 uses 128-bit addresses to accommodate the growing number of connected devices.

6. What is a subnet mask, and how is it used in IP addressing and routing?

Answer: A subnet mask is used to divide an IP address into network and host portions. It helps routers determine which part of an IP address is the network and which is the host, aiding in routing decisions.

7. What is a MAC address, and how does it differ from an IP address?

Answer: A MAC (Media Access Control) address is a hardware-based, unique identifier for network interfaces. It operates at the data link layer, while an IP address is used for routing data at the network layer.

8. What is DNS, and why is it an essential part of the internet?

Answer: DNS (Domain Name System) is a system that translates human-readable domain names into IP addresses. It's crucial for making internet resources accessible through easy-to-remember domain names.

9. What is the purpose of firewalls in network security, and how do they work to protect networks?

Answer: Firewalls are network security devices that filter traffic based on predetermined security rules. They help protect networks by blocking unauthorized access, preventing threats, and monitoring traffic for malicious activity.

10. Explain the concept of bandwidth and latency in networking and their impact on network performance.

Answer: Bandwidth refers to the data transfer rate of a network, while latency is the time it takes for data to travel from the source to the destination. Both affect network performance: higher bandwidth allows for faster data transfer, while lower latency results in quicker response times.

Distributed File Systems

1. What is a distributed file system, and how does it differ from a traditional centralized file system?

Answer: A distributed file system is a network-based file system that allows files to be stored and accessed across multiple servers or nodes. It differs from a traditional centralized file system by distributing data across multiple locations, often for improved performance and fault tolerance.

2. Explain the concept of data transparency in distributed file systems and its significance.

Answer: Data transparency in distributed file systems means that users and applications can access files without being aware of their physical location or how they are distributed. It ensures simplicity, consistency, and ease of use.

3. What is data replication in distributed file systems, and how does it contribute to fault tolerance and performance?

Answer: Data replication involves creating duplicate copies of files across multiple nodes. It enhances fault tolerance by allowing data recovery in case of node failures and improves performance by enabling parallel access to data.

4. What challenges are associated with maintaining data consistency in distributed file systems, and how are they addressed?

Answer: Challenges include concurrent access, network delays, and node failures. Data consistency is maintained using techniques like distributed locks, transactions, and version control to ensure that data remains coherent across distributed nodes.

5. Explain the role of a distributed file system's naming service in managing file access and addressing in a networked environment.

Answer: The naming service maps user-friendly file names to their physical locations in a distributed file system. It simplifies file access and enables users to work with files using familiar names rather than complex addresses.

6. How do distributed file systems handle file access permissions and security in a networked environment?

Answer: Distributed file systems employ access control mechanisms to manage file permissions, ensuring that only authorized users can read, write, or execute files. They also use encryption and authentication to secure data during transmission.

7. What is the significance of caching in distributed file systems, and how does it improve performance?

Answer: Caching involves storing frequently accessed data in memory. It improves performance by reducing the need for repeated network requests and minimizing data transfer times.

8. Explain the role of file locking mechanisms in distributed file systems and how they prevent data inconsistencies.

Answer: File locking mechanisms ensure that only one process can modify a file at a time. They prevent data inconsistencies by serializing write operations and ensuring that changes do not overlap.

9. What is the purpose of load balancing in distributed file systems, and how does it improve system performance?

Answer: Load balancing evenly distributes file access requests across distributed nodes, preventing overloading of any single node. It improves system performance by maximizing resource utilization and reducing response times.

10. How do distributed file systems manage metadata, and why is metadata management essential for file system operation?

Answer: Metadata in a distributed file system includes information about files, their attributes, and their locations. Proper metadata management is essential for file system operation, as it ensures accurate file tracking, efficient search and retrieval, and overall system organization.

Distributed Process Management

1. What is distributed process management, and why is it important in distributed systems?

Answer: Distributed process management involves the coordination and control of processes running on multiple nodes in a distributed system. It is essential for efficient resource utilization, fault tolerance, and parallel processing.

2. Explain the concept of process migration in distributed systems and its use cases.

Answer: Process migration allows a running process to be moved from one node to another. Use cases include load balancing, resource optimization, and fault tolerance.

3. How does distributed process management handle process communication and synchronization across multiple nodes in a networked environment?

Answer: Distributed process management uses inter-process communication (IPC) mechanisms, such as message passing and remote procedure calls, for communication and synchronization between processes on different nodes.

4. What are the challenges in ensuring data consistency and synchronization when processes run on different nodes in a distributed system?

Answer: Challenges include network latency, concurrent access, and node failures. Distributed systems use techniques like distributed locks, transactions, and version control to maintain data consistency.

5. Explain the role of process monitoring in distributed systems and how it contributes to fault tolerance.

Answer: Process monitoring involves tracking the health and status of processes. It contributes to fault tolerance by allowing the system to detect and recover from process failures.

6. What is process coordination, and how does it improve the efficiency of distributed systems?

Answer: Process coordination involves managing the order and dependencies of processes in a distributed environment. It improves system efficiency by ensuring processes are executed in a logical sequence and that their results are consistent.

7. What are distributed scheduling algorithms, and how do they influence the allocation of processes in a networked environment?

Answer: Distributed scheduling algorithms determine the assignment of processes to nodes. They aim to optimize resource utilization, load balancing, and system responsiveness.

8. How does distributed process management ensure data security and privacy in a distributed system?

Answer: Distributed process management uses encryption, authentication, and access control mechanisms to secure data during process communication and storage. It also restricts access to sensitive data.

9. Explain the concept of distributed deadlock detection in a distributed system and its importance.

Answer: Distributed deadlock detection identifies and resolves deadlocks that may occur when multiple processes compete for resources across nodes. It is crucial for preventing system hang-ups and ensuring the continuous operation of distributed systems.

10. What is process fault tolerance, and how do distributed systems implement it to ensure system reliability?

Answer: Process fault tolerance involves designing processes to continue functioning even in the presence of failures. Distributed systems use techniques like redundancy, replication, and process recovery to achieve fault tolerance and maintain system reliability.

Distributed Security

1. What is distributed security, and why is it crucial in networked systems?

Answer: Distributed security refers to the measures and protocols put in place to protect data and resources across multiple interconnected nodes. It is vital to ensure the confidentiality, integrity, and availability of data and services in a distributed environment.

2. Explain the concept of end-to-end encryption in distributed security and its role in data protection.

Answer: End-to-end encryption ensures that data is encrypted at the source and only decrypted at the destination, providing confidentiality during transit. It safeguards data from eavesdropping or interception.

3. What is a Distributed Denial of Service (DDoS) attack, and how can distributed security mechanisms mitigate its impact?

Answer: A DDoS attack involves overwhelming a target with a flood of traffic from multiple sources. Distributed security measures, such as traffic filtering and load balancing, can help mitigate the impact of DDoS attacks.

4. Explain the principle of access control in distributed security and how it regulates resource access across distributed nodes.

Answer: Access control specifies who can access resources and what actions they can perform. It regulates resource access and helps prevent unauthorized users or processes from compromising the security of a distributed system.

5. What is the role of public-key infrastructure (PKI) in distributed security, and how does it support secure communication?

Answer: PKI provides a framework for managing digital certificates and encryption keys. It enables secure authentication, data encryption, and digital signatures, ensuring the integrity and authenticity of data in distributed systems.

6. How do distributed systems use network segmentation as a security measure, and why is it effective?

Answer: Network segmentation involves dividing a network into smaller, isolated segments. It helps contain security breaches by restricting lateral movement within the network and limiting the potential impact of attacks.

7. What are the security challenges associated with managing and securing user identities in distributed systems?

Answer: Challenges include identity management, user authentication, and single sign-on (SSO). Distributed security systems use techniques like federated identity management and multi-factor authentication to address these challenges.

8. Explain the concept of intrusion detection systems (IDS) and intrusion prevention systems (IPS) in the context of distributed security.

Answer: IDS monitors network traffic for suspicious activity, while IPS can take action to block or mitigate potential threats. Together, they provide real-time threat detection and response in distributed systems.

What are zero-trust security models, and how do they enhance security in distributed environments?

Answer: Zero-trust security models assume that no entity is inherently trusted, and access must be continuously verified. They enhance security in distributed systems by ensuring that all network segments and users are subject to strict access controls.

Explain the role of security policies and compliance in distributed security, and how do they ensure adherence to security best practices?

Answer: Security policies define the rules, guidelines, and procedures for securing a distributed system. Compliance ensures that the system adheres to these policies and meets regulatory and industry-specific security standards.

ONLINE RESOURCES

Practice Paper Link: **https://forms.gle/CD6jG2fk5sABAL3h8**

QR Code:

Video Link: **https://www.youtube.com/playlist?list=PLzlh_31VWEFq-auuAtOHhZfCMKEeKtrb8**

QR Code:

Chapter 8: Security and Protection

Threats and Security Goals

1. What are the primary security goals in computer and network security, and why are they important?

Answer: The primary security goals are confidentiality, integrity, availability, and authenticity. These goals ensure that data remains private, unaltered, accessible when needed, and originates from a trusted source.

2. Explain the concept of confidentiality as a security goal. How is it achieved in information security?

Answer: Confidentiality ensures that sensitive information is accessible only to authorized users. It is achieved through encryption, access controls, and data classification.

3. What is the security goal of integrity, and how can data integrity be maintained in a networked environment?

Answer: Integrity ensures that data is not tampered with or altered in an unauthorized manner. Maintaining data integrity involves using checksums, hashing, digital signatures, and access controls to prevent unauthorized changes.

4. Why is availability a critical security goal, and what measures are taken to ensure system availability in the face of threats?

Answer: Availability ensures that systems and data are accessible when needed. It is crucial to prevent disruptions due to attacks or failures. Measures include redundancy, failover systems, and disaster recovery plans.

5. What is the importance of authenticity as a security goal, and how does authentication contribute to achieving it?

Answer: Authenticity verifies that data or communications originate from a trusted source. Authentication mechanisms like passwords, biometrics, and digital certificates help confirm the identity of users and systems.

6. Explain the term "threat" in the context of security. What are some common types of threats in computer and network security?

Answer: A threat is any potential danger that could exploit a vulnerability to breach security and harm an organization. Common threats include malware, phishing, insider threats, and denial of service attacks.

7. How does the CIA triad (Confidentiality, Integrity, Availability) help organizations in setting security goals and prioritizing security measures?

Answer: The CIA triad provides a framework for organizations to define, assess, and prioritize security goals and measures. It guides them in balancing the three core security objectives based on their specific needs and risks.

8. What is the concept of a "zero-day vulnerability," and how does it pose a significant threat to computer and network security?

Answer: A zero-day vulnerability is a security flaw in software or hardware that is exploited by attackers before the vendor has released a fix (a "zero-day" exploit). These vulnerabilities pose a significant threat because they are unknown and unpatched, making them attractive targets for attackers.

9. What are some social engineering threats, and how can organizations defend against them?

Answer: Social engineering threats involve manipulating individuals into divulging confidential information. Defense strategies include security awareness training, user education, and strict access controls.

10. Explain the concept of defense-in-depth as a security strategy. How does it address various types of threats and security goals?

Answer: Defense-in-depth involves employing multiple layers of security measures to protect against a variety of threats. It addresses security goals by providing redundancy and multiple barriers to breaches, enhancing overall security posture.

Authentication and Access Control

1. What is authentication in the context of computer security, and why is it important?

Answer: Authentication is the process of verifying the identity of a user or system. It is crucial for ensuring that only authorized individuals or entities gain access to resources and data.

2. Explain the difference between authentication and authorization.

Answer: Authentication verifies the identity of a user, while authorization determines what actions or resources that authenticated user is allowed to access.

3. What are the three primary factors in multi-factor authentication (MFA), and how does it enhance security?

Answer: The three factors in MFA are something you know (e.g., a password), something you have (e.g., a smartphone), and something you are (e.g., a fingerprint). MFA enhances security by requiring multiple forms of authentication, making it more difficult for unauthorized users to gain access.

4. What is a password policy, and what are some key elements that organizations should consider when implementing one?

Answer: A password policy outlines rules for creating, using, and managing passwords. Key elements include password complexity requirements, regular password changes, and password storage and protection.

5. Explain the concept of biometric authentication, and provide examples of biometric identifiers.

Answer: Biometric authentication uses physical or behavioural characteristics to verify identity. Examples of biometric identifiers include fingerprints, facial recognition, iris scans, and voice recognition.

6. What is role-based access control (RBAC), and how does it help organizations manage access to resources?

Answer: RBAC assigns roles to users or groups and specifies what actions they can perform based on those roles. It simplifies access control and minimizes the risk of unauthorized access.

7. What is the principle of least privilege, and why is it a fundamental concept in access control?

Answer: The principle of least privilege dictates that users and systems should only have the minimum access necessary to perform their tasks. It minimizes potential security risks and limits the damage that can be caused by compromised accounts.

8. Explain the difference between discretionary access control (DAC) and mandatory access control (MAC).

Answer:

DAC allows users to determine access permissions to their own resources.

MAC is centrally administered and enforces access policies defined by the system's security administrator.

9. What is access control lists (ACLs), and how are they used to manage resource access?

Answer: ACLs are lists of permissions attached to a resource, specifying which users or system entities can access it and what actions they can perform. They are used to control access to files, directories, or network resources.

10. What is the significance of auditing and logging in authentication and access control, and how do they aid in security monitoring and incident response?

Answer: Auditing and logging record access and authentication events, helping organizations monitor for suspicious activity and aiding in incident response and forensic analysis. They provide an audit trail for identifying security breaches and policy violations.

Cryptography

1. What is cryptography, and why is it important in the field of computer security?

Answer: Cryptography is the science of securing communication and information by encoding data to protect its confidentiality, integrity, and authenticity. It plays a vital role in safeguarding sensitive information in computer security.

2. Explain the difference between encryption and decryption in the context of cryptography.

Answer: Encryption is the process of converting plaintext data into ciphertext, while decryption is the process of converting ciphertext back into plaintext, using an encryption algorithm and a decryption key.

3. What is the difference between symmetric and asymmetric cryptography, and when should each be used?

Answer: Symmetric cryptography uses a single key for both encryption and decryption, while asymmetric cryptography uses a pair of public and private keys. Symmetric encryption is faster and should be used for data transmission, while asymmetric encryption is more secure and is typically used for key exchange and digital signatures.

4. What is the role of a cryptographic algorithm, and what characteristics are desirable in a secure encryption algorithm?

Answer: A cryptographic algorithm defines the mathematical operations used for encryption and decryption. Desirable characteristics in a secure encryption algorithm include confidentiality, integrity, non-repudiation, and resistance to attacks.

5. Explain the concept of a cryptographic key and how it relates to the security of encrypted data.

Answer: A cryptographic key is a parameter used by the encryption algorithm to transform plaintext into ciphertext. The security of encrypted data relies on the secrecy and strength of the encryption key.

6. What is a digital signature, and how does it provide data integrity and authenticity in electronic communication?

Answer: A digital signature is a cryptographic technique that verifies the origin and integrity of digital messages or documents. It uses the private key of the sender to create a unique signature, which can be verified using the sender's public key.

7. Explain the purpose of a cryptographic hash function and how it is used in computer security.

Answer: A cryptographic hash function transforms data into a fixed-size hash value. It is used to verify data integrity, create digital signatures, and securely store passwords.

8. What is a public key infrastructure (PKI), and how does it support secure communication in a networked environment?

Answer: A PKI is a framework for managing digital keys and certificates. It supports secure communication by providing authentication, encryption, and digital signatures, ensuring data integrity and authenticity.

9. What are some common encryption algorithms and their use cases in computer security?

Answer: Common encryption algorithms include AES for symmetric encryption, RSA for asymmetric encryption, and SHA-256 for cryptographic hashing. AES is used for data encryption, RSA for key exchange, and SHA-256 for data integrity.

10. What is the concept of a "man-in-the-middle" attack, and how can encryption and authentication mechanisms mitigate this threat?

Answer: A man-in-the-middle attack involves an attacker intercepting communication between two parties. Encryption and authentication mechanisms help mitigate this threat by ensuring the confidentiality and authenticity of data, making it difficult for an attacker to intercept or alter the communication.

Malware and Virus Protection

1. What is malware, and why is it a significant concern for computer security?

Answer: Malware is malicious software designed to disrupt, damage, or gain unauthorized access to computer systems. It's a significant concern because it can lead to data loss, system instability, and security breaches.

2. Explain the differences between viruses, worms, Trojans, and ransomware.

Answer:

Viruses attach themselves to legitimate programs and replicate when the program is run.

Worms are standalone and spread through network vulnerabilities.

Trojans disguise themselves as legitimate software.

Ransomware encrypts data and demands a ransom for decryption.

3. What is the role of antivirus software, and how does it protect against malware?

Answer: Antivirus software detects and removes malware from a computer. It does this by scanning files and processes for known malware signatures and suspicious behaviour.

4. Explain the concept of heuristic analysis in antivirus software and its importance in detecting new and unknown threats.

Answer: Heuristic analysis involves identifying potential threats based on their behaviour and characteristics. It's important for detecting new and unknown threats that may not have known signatures.

5. What is real-time scanning in antivirus software, and how does it enhance malware protection?

Answer: Real-time scanning continuously monitors files and processes for malware as they are accessed or executed. It enhances malware protection by preventing malware from gaining a foothold on the system.

6. What is the significance of keeping software and operating systems up to date in malware prevention?

Answer: Updating software and operating systems is crucial to patch security vulnerabilities that malware can exploit. Regular updates reduce the attack surface and enhance overall system security.

7. Explain the role of firewalls in malware protection and how they help block unauthorized network traffic.

Answer: Firewalls filter incoming and outgoing network traffic, allowing only authorized communication. They help block malware from infiltrating the network and prevent malware from sending data out.

8. What are best practices for safe internet browsing and email usage to avoid malware infections?

Answer: Best practices include being cautious with email attachments and links, avoiding suspicious websites, keeping browser and email client software updated, and using ad blockers and script blockers.

9. What is sandboxing, and how does it protect against malware infections?

Answer: Sandboxing is the practice of running untrusted or potentially malicious software in an isolated environment. It protects against malware infections by containing the threat within the sandbox, preventing it from affecting the host system.

10. Explain the importance of regular data backups in mitigating the impact of malware attacks.

Answer: Regular data backups are crucial in case of a malware infection or data loss. They allow you to restore your system and data to a previous state, reducing the impact of an attack and preventing data loss.

Security Policies and Models

1. What is a security policy, and why is it an essential component of an organization's security strategy?

Answer: A security policy is a set of guidelines and rules that define how an organization protects its assets and information. It is essential because it establishes the framework for security, helps in compliance, and guides employees in secure practices.

2. Explain the difference between a security policy, a standard, and a procedure.

Answer:

A security policy is a high-level statement of security objectives.

A security standard is a specific requirement or control to meet those objectives.

A security procedure is a step-by-step guide for implementing standards.

3. What are the key elements that a comprehensive security policy should cover, and why are they important?

Answer: A comprehensive security policy should cover access control, data protection, incident response, and compliance. These elements are important because they address the key aspects of security governance and risk management.

4. Explain the purpose of a data classification policy, and how does it help in safeguarding sensitive information?

Answer: A data classification policy categorizes data based on its sensitivity and importance. It helps in safeguarding sensitive information by ensuring that appropriate security controls are applied based on the data's classification.

5. What is the principle of least privilege (PoLP), and how does it relate to access control policies?

Answer: The principle of least privilege restricts users and systems to the minimum level of access required to perform their tasks. Access control policies should implement PoLP to reduce the risk of unauthorized access.

6. Explain the concept of role-based access control (RBAC) and its role in access management.

Answer: RBAC assigns permissions based on user roles or job functions. It simplifies access control by grouping users and systems according to their responsibilities and granting access accordingly.

7. What is the Bell-LaPadula model, and how does it enforce confidentiality in security policies?

Answer: The Bell-LaPadula model is a security model that enforces confidentiality by defining access controls based on security labels and access rules, ensuring that information cannot flow from higher to lower security levels.

8. What is the difference between a top-down security policy and a bottom-up security policy, and when is each approach appropriate?

Answer: A top-down security policy is developed at the executive level and trickles down to lower levels of the organization.

A bottom-up security policy is created by lower-level staff and proposed upwards. The approach chosen depends on the organization's structure, culture, and security needs.

9. Explain the importance of regular policy reviews and updates in maintaining effective security policies.

Answer: Regular policy reviews and updates are important to ensure that security policies remain aligned with changing business needs, evolving threats, and emerging technologies, and to adapt to new compliance requirements.

10. What is the ISO 27001 standard, and how can it be used to develop a comprehensive security policy framework?

Answer: ISO 27001 is an international standard for information security management systems (ISMS). It can be used to develop a comprehensive security policy framework by providing a structured approach to information security that covers risk assessment, controls, monitoring, and continuous improvement.

ONLINE RESOURCES

Practice Paper Link: https://forms.gle/mirFEK9cmiGSPfyA9

QR Code:

Video Link: https://www.youtube.com/playlist?list=PLzlh_31VWEFpVk0I2Ux9gausDx0oTYDru

QR Code:

Chapter 9: Virtualization and Cloud Computing

Virtualization Concepts

1. What is virtualization, and how does it differ from traditional physical computing?

Answer: Virtualization is the process of creating virtual instances of resources, such as servers, storage, or networks, to abstract and share physical resources. It differs from traditional physical computing by enabling multiple virtual environments on a single physical infrastructure.

2. Explain the concept of a virtual machine (VM) and its benefits in a virtualized environment.

Answer: A virtual machine is a software-based emulation of a physical computer. It enables running multiple operating systems and applications on a single physical server, providing flexibility, resource optimization, and isolation.

3. What are hypervisors, and what are the two main types of hypervisors commonly used in virtualization?

Answer: Hypervisors are software or hardware platforms that create and manage virtual machines. The two main types are Type 1 (bare-metal) hypervisors that run directly on the hardware (e.g., VMware ESXi) and Type 2 (hosted) hypervisors that run on a conventional operating system (e.g., VMware Workstation).

4. Explain the concept of containerization and how it differs from traditional virtualization.

Answer: Containerization is a lightweight form of virtualization that packages an application and its dependencies into a single container. Unlike traditional virtualization, it doesn't require a separate operating system for each container, making it more efficient.

5. What is the significance of resource pooling and dynamic resource allocation in virtualization?

Answer: Resource pooling involves aggregating physical resources to be shared by virtual instances. Dynamic resource allocation allows resources to be allocated based on demand, improving resource utilization and scalability.

6. How does virtualization enhance disaster recovery and business continuity strategies?

Answer: Virtualization allows for the creation of virtual backups or snapshots of entire virtual machines, making disaster recovery faster and more efficient. In case of a hardware failure, virtual machines can be quickly migrated to other available hardware.

7. Explain the concept of live migration in virtualization and its use in load balancing and maintenance.

Answer: Live migration enables moving a running virtual machine from one host to another without interrupting its operation. It is used for load balancing to distribute workloads evenly and for maintenance to avoid downtime during hardware upgrades.

8. What is the "virtualization overhead," and how can it impact system performance?

Answer: Virtualization overhead refers to the additional processing required to manage virtualization. While modern virtualization solutions have minimal overhead, it can impact system performance, especially when virtual machines are resource-intensive.

9. What are some security considerations in a virtualized environment, and how can they be addressed?

Answer: Security considerations include VM isolation, vulnerabilities in hypervisors, and improper configuration. Addressing them involves implementing proper access controls, patch management, and network segmentation.

10. Explain the concept of software-defined networking (SDN) and how it complements virtualization in data centers.

Answer: SDN is a network architecture that separates the control plane from the data plane, making network management more flexible and programmable. It complements virtualization by allowing dynamic network configuration to meet the changing needs of virtual environments.

Virtual Machines

1. What is a virtual machine (VM), and how does it differ from a physical machine?

Answer: A virtual machine is a software emulation of a physical computer that runs an operating system and applications. It differs from a physical machine in that it shares hardware resources with other VMs on the same host, allowing multiple VMs to run on a single physical server.

2. What are the primary benefits of using virtual machines in a data center or cloud environment?

Answer: VMs offer benefits such as resource consolidation, improved resource utilization, easy migration and backup, isolation, and flexibility in running multiple operating systems and applications on a single physical server.

3. Explain the role of a hypervisor in managing virtual machines.

Answer: A hypervisor is a software or hardware platform that creates and manages virtual machines. It allocates physical resources to VMs, isolates them from each other, and enables the execution of multiple VMs on a single host.

4. What are Type 1 and Type 2 hypervisors, and how do they differ in their implementation?

Answer:Type 1 hypervisors run directly on the host's hardware (bare-metal), while Type 2 hypervisors run on top of a conventional operating system. Type 1 hypervisors typically provide better performance and security.

5. What is the purpose of a snapshot in virtualization, and how is it different from a backup?

Answer: A snapshot is a point-in-time image of a VM's state. It is used for capturing the VM's configuration and data at a specific moment. Snapshots are different from backups, as they are not intended for long-term data retention or full recovery but rather for quickly restoring to a known state.

6. Explain the concept of virtual CPU (vCPU) and how it differs from a physical CPU core.

Answer: A virtual CPU (vCPU) is a CPU assigned to a virtual machine. It differs from a physical CPU core in that multiple vCPUs may be scheduled to run on the same physical core. vCPUs are time-sliced to provide processing power to multiple VMs.

7. What is live migration in virtualization, and what are its benefits in a data center environment?

Answer: Live migration allows the movement of a running VM from one host to another without causing downtime. It benefits data centers by enabling load balancing, hardware maintenance without service disruption, and improved resource management.

8. What is ballooning in virtualization, and how does it help manage memory resources?

Answer: Ballooning is a memory management technique where a balloon driver inside the guest VM allocates or deallocates memory to help balance memory usage across VMs on the same host, ensuring efficient resource utilization.

9. Explain the term "overcommitting" in virtualization and how it relates to resource allocation.

Answer: Overcommitting involves allocating more resources (e.g., CPU, memory) to VMs than are physically available on the host. It relies on the assumption that not all VMs will demand their allocated resources simultaneously, allowing for higher resource utilization.

10. What are some security considerations when using virtual machines, and how can they be addressed?

Answer: Security considerations include VM isolation, vulnerabilities in hypervisors, and data leakage. Addressing these concerns involves configuring strong access controls, keeping hypervisors updated, and implementing network segmentation to prevent unauthorized access to VMs.

Hypervisors

1. What is a hypervisor, and what is its primary role in virtualization?

Answer: A hypervisor is a software or hardware platform that creates and manages virtual machines (VMs). Its primary role is to allocate and manage physical resources to multiple VMs while providing isolation between them.

2. Explain the difference between Type 1 and Type 2 hypervisors.

Answer:

Type 1 hypervisors run directly on the host hardware, providing better performance and security. Examples include VMware ESXi and Microsoft Hyper-V.

Type 2 hypervisors run on top of a conventional operating system and are typically used for development and testing. Examples include VMware Workstation and Oracle VirtualBox.

3. What are the benefits of using a Type 1 hypervisor in a data center or cloud environment?

Answer: Type 1 hypervisors offer benefits like improved performance, direct access to physical resources, and better security, making them ideal for large-scale data center deployments.

4. How does a hypervisor handle the allocation of CPU and memory resources to virtual machines?

Answer: A hypervisor schedules vCPUs (virtual CPUs) and manages memory allocation to VMs based on their resource requirements. It ensures fair access and prevents resource contention.

5. Explain the concept of live migration in the context of hypervisors and its use in load balancing.

Answer: Live migration allows a running VM to be moved from one physical host to another without service disruption. It is used for load balancing, hardware maintenance, and ensuring high availability.

6. What is the purpose of paravirtualization, and how does it improve VM performance?

Answer: Paravirtualization is a technique where the guest operating system is modified to work closely with the hypervisor. This improves VM performance by reducing the overhead of emulation.

7. What is hardware virtualization assist, and how does it enhance the performance of virtual machines?

Answer: Hardware virtualization assist (e.g., Intel VT-x, AMD-V) is a technology that offloads virtualization tasks to the CPU. It improves VM performance by reducing the overhead associated with software-based virtualization.

8. Explain the role of the virtual machine monitor (VMM) in a Type 1 hypervisor.

Answer: The VMM, also known as the hypervisor, is responsible for managing and controlling the execution of VMs. It intercepts and manages the interactions between VMs and the underlying hardware.

9. What are the security considerations when using hypervisors, and how can they be addressed?

Answer: Security considerations include VM isolation, vulnerabilities in the hypervisor, and resource contention. They can be addressed through proper access controls, regular hypervisor updates, and network segmentation.

10. What is the significance of resource management and optimization in hypervisor-based virtualization?

Answer: Resource management and optimization are crucial for ensuring that VMs receive the necessary resources, preventing resource bottlenecks, and optimizing overall system performance in virtualized environments.

Cloud Computing Models

1. What are the three primary cloud computing service models, and how do they differ from each other?

Answer: The three primary cloud service models are Infrastructure as a Service (IaaS), Platform as a Service (PaaS), and Software as a Service (SaaS).

IaaS provides virtualized infrastructure resources.

PaaS offers a platform for application development and deployment.

SaaS delivers software applications over the internet.

2. Explain the concept of Infrastructure as a Service (IaaS) and provide an example of IaaS providers.

Answer: IaaS delivers virtualized computing resources, such as virtual machines, storage, and networking. Examples of IaaS providers include Amazon Web Services (AWS), Microsoft Azure, and Google Cloud Platform (GCP).

3. What is the primary advantage of Platform as a Service (PaaS), and how does it streamline application development and deployment?

Answer: The primary advantage of PaaS is that it abstracts infrastructure management, allowing developers to focus on coding and application logic. PaaS provides tools and frameworks for building, testing, and deploying applications.

4. Explain the benefits of Software as a Service (SaaS) for end-users and organizations.

Answer: SaaS offers benefits like easy access to software without installation, automatic updates, and cost savings. For organizations, it reduces the burden of software maintenance and infrastructure management.

5. What is the key difference between public, private, and hybrid cloud deployment models?

Answer:

Public cloud is hosted and managed by a cloud service provider, accessible to the public.

Private cloud is dedicated to a single organization and may be hosted on-premises or by a third-party provider.

Hybrid cloud combines both public and private clouds, offering flexibility and scalability.

6. Explain the concept of serverless computing and how it differs from traditional cloud computing models.

Answer: Serverless computing allows developers to run code without managing servers. It automatically scales based on demand, and users are billed only for the resources used during code execution.

7. What are the challenges and considerations in selecting a cloud deployment model for an organization?

Answer: Challenges and considerations include data security, compliance, cost, performance, and workload suitability. Organizations need to assess their specific requirements and objectives when choosing a cloud model.

8. What is containerization in the context of cloud computing, and how does it benefit application deployment and scalability?

Answer: Containerization is the process of packaging applications and their dependencies into lightweight, consistent units called containers. It benefits application deployment by ensuring consistency across environments and enhancing scalability.

9. Explain the concept of server virtualization in cloud computing and its role in optimizing resource utilization.

Answer: Server virtualization involves running multiple virtual machines on a single physical server. It optimizes resource utilization by allowing multiple workloads to share the same hardware.

10. What is edge computing, and how does it extend cloud computing to the network's edge?

Answer: Edge computing is a distributed computing paradigm that brings computation and data storage closer to the data source or endpoint. It extends cloud computing by reducing latency and enabling real-time processing at the network's edge.

Cloud Service Providers

1. What are cloud service providers (CSPs), and how do they fit into the cloud computing ecosystem?

Answer: Cloud service providers are companies that offer cloud computing services, including infrastructure, platform, and software services. They provide the underlying technology and infrastructure for cloud computing.

2. Name some of the leading public cloud service providers and briefly describe their areas of expertise.

Answer: Leading public cloud service providers include Amazon Web Services (AWS), Microsoft Azure, Google Cloud Platform (GCP), and IBM Cloud.

AWS excels in providing a wide range of services, from computing to artificial intelligence.

Azure is strong in hybrid cloud solutions and enterprise integration.

GCP is known for its data analytics and machine learning capabilities.

IBM Cloud specializes in hybrid and multicloud deployments.

3. What are the key factors organizations should consider when selecting a cloud service provider for their specific needs?

Answer: Organizations should consider factors such as cost, performance, security, compliance, scalability, and the specific services offered by the provider. The choice depends on the organization's requirements and priorities.

4. Explain the concept of cloud regions and availability zones within a cloud service provider's infrastructure.

Answer: A cloud region is a geographic area where a CSP hosts its services, while availability zones are data centers within a region. Availability zones offer redundancy and failover capabilities.

5. What is the significance of service-level agreements (SLAs) in cloud computing, and how do they vary among different cloud service providers?

Answer: SLAs define the terms and conditions for the services provided by a CSP. They specify performance guarantees, uptime, and support levels. SLAs can vary significantly among providers, so it's crucial to understand the specific terms and commitments.

6. Explain the concept of serverless computing and how various cloud providers offer serverless solutions.

Answer: Serverless computing allows developers to run code without managing server infrastructure. Different cloud providers offer serverless solutions, such as AWS Lambda, Azure Functions, and Google Cloud Functions, which automatically scale and charge only for actual execution.

7. What are the advantages of multicloud and hybrid cloud strategies, and how do cloud service providers facilitate these approaches?

Answer: Multicloud and hybrid cloud strategies offer redundancy, flexibility, and the ability to meet specific regulatory or compliance requirements. Cloud providers often have solutions and services that enable multicloud and hybrid deployments.

8. What are the typical pricing models offered by cloud service providers, and how do they impact an organization's cloud costs?

Answer: Cloud providers offer various pricing models, including pay-as-you-go, reserved instances, and spot instances. Organizations must carefully choose the pricing model that aligns with their usage patterns to optimize costs.

9. Explain the role of cloud marketplaces in cloud service provider ecosystems and how they benefit customers.

Answer: Cloud marketplaces offer a variety of pre-configured applications, services, and solutions that customers can easily deploy. They simplify software procurement and deployment in the cloud.

10. How do cloud service providers address data security and compliance concerns, and what are some common security features and tools they offer?

Answer: Cloud providers offer robust security features, including encryption, identity and access management, monitoring, and compliance certifications. They also provide tools for organizations to implement security and compliance controls within their cloud environments.

ONLINE RESOURCES

Practice Paper: https://forms.gle/YsyAtzMFisRj9wLeA

QR Code:

Video Link: https://www.youtube.com/playlist?list=PLzlh_31VWEFof7DpbLyhvLatMoborYWz8

QR Code:

Chapter 10: Trends and Emerging Technologies

Containerization

1. What is containerization, and how does it differ from traditional virtualization?

Answer: Containerization is a lightweight form of virtualization that allows applications and their dependencies to run in isolated environments. It differs from traditional virtualization in that it shares the host OS kernel, making it more efficient and portable.

2. What is a container image, and how does it facilitate the deployment of applications in containers?

Answer: A container image is a standalone package that includes the application code, runtime, libraries, and system tools. It simplifies the deployment process by ensuring consistency across environments.

3. Explain the role of a container runtime, and provide an example of a popular container runtime.

Answer: A container runtime is responsible for executing containers. Docker is a popular container runtime that manages container creation, execution, and networking.

4. What is the difference between a container and a virtual machine (VM), and when should you use one over the other?

Answer: Containers share the host OS kernel, making them more lightweight and faster to start than VMs, which run their own OS. Containers are suitable for microservices and applications with minimal resource requirements, while VMs are better for running multiple applications with diverse OS needs.

5. Explain the concept of container orchestration and the role of orchestration platforms like Kubernetes.

Answer: Container orchestration involves managing, scaling, and automating the deployment of containers. Kubernetes is an example of an orchestration platform that simplifies the management of containerized applications across a cluster of machines.

6. What is containerization's impact on resource utilization and system efficiency compared to running applications directly on a host OS?

Answer: Containerization can improve resource utilization by allowing applications to share the same OS kernel, reducing overhead and optimizing system efficiency.

7. How does containerization aid in application portability, and what are some common container registries for storing and sharing container images?

Answer: Containerization provides application portability by packaging applications and dependencies in a consistent manner. Common container registries include Docker Hub, Google Container Registry, and Amazon Elastic Container Registry (ECR).

8. Explain the advantages of containerization for microservices architecture and cloud-native applications.

Answer: Containerization is well-suited for microservices architecture and cloud-native applications because it enables rapid development, scaling, and simplified management of individual components or services.

9. What are security considerations when using containers, and how can these concerns be addressed?

Answer: Security considerations include container image vulnerabilities, isolation, and access controls. To address these concerns, use trusted images, restrict container permissions, and implement security measures such as container security scanners.

10. What are some alternative container runtimes to Docker, and why might organizations choose them over Docker?

Answer: Alternative container runtimes include containerd and rkt (pronounced "rocket"). Organizations might choose these alternatives for their simplicity, compatibility with container standards, and reduced attack surface.

Internet of Things (IoT)

1. What is the Internet of Things (IoT), and how does it relate to operating systems?

Answer: IoT refers to the network of physical devices, vehicles, buildings, and other objects embedded with sensors, software, and network connectivity. Operating systems play a crucial role in managing and controlling these devices.

2. Explain the concept of edge computing in IoT and its importance in operating systems.

Answer: Edge computing in IoT involves processing data closer to the data source, reducing latency and bandwidth usage. Operating systems on edge devices manage this local data processing and communication.

3. What are some challenges in implementing real-time operating systems (RTOS) for IoT devices, and how do they differ from general-purpose operating systems?

Answer: RTOS for IoT devices need to handle real-time constraints, low power consumption, and resource constraints. They differ from general-purpose OSs by prioritizing predictability and efficiency over versatility.

4. How do operating systems in IoT devices manage power consumption and extend battery life?

Answer: IoT operating systems use power management techniques such as sleep modes and dynamic voltage scaling to reduce power consumption during idle periods, extending battery life.

5. What is the role of wireless communication protocols in IoT, and how do operating systems enable device connectivity through these protocols?

Answer: Wireless communication protocols like Wi-Fi, Bluetooth, and LoRaWAN are essential for IoT connectivity. Operating systems include drivers and stacks that support these protocols, enabling device communication.

6. Explain the concept of IoT security, and how do operating systems contribute to securing IoT devices and data?

Answer: IoT security involves protecting devices, data, and communications. Operating systems provide security features like encryption, access controls, and secure boot processes to safeguard IoT devices.

7. What is over-the-air (OTA) firmware updating, and how does it benefit IoT devices?

Answer: OTA firmware updating allows IoT devices to receive software updates remotely. This feature is crucial for patching vulnerabilities, adding new features, and improving device performance.

8. How does IoT device management work, and what role do operating systems play in device provisioning, monitoring, and maintenance?

Answer: IoT device management involves provisioning, monitoring, and maintaining devices throughout their lifecycle. Operating systems help facilitate these processes by providing management interfaces and capabilities.

9. Explain the concept of IoT data processing at the edge, and how operating systems support local data analytics.

Answer: Edge data processing involves analyzing data locally on IoT devices before sending it to the cloud. Operating systems enable this by supporting lightweight data processing and analytics tools.

10. What are the scalability challenges in managing a large number of IoT devices, and how do operating systems help address them?

Answer: Managing a vast number of IoT devices can be challenging. Operating systems support device management solutions that automate tasks, monitor device health, and enable scalability in IoT deployments.

Edge Computing

1. What is edge computing, and how does it differ from traditional cloud computing?

Answer: Edge computing is a decentralized computing paradigm that processes data closer to the data source, reducing latency. It differs from traditional cloud computing, which relies on centralized data centers for processing.

2. Explain the concept of an "edge device" and provide examples of devices that can serve as edges in an edge computing network.

Answer: An edge device is a device at the edge of the network that processes data locally. Examples include IoT devices, routers, gateways, and industrial controllers.

3. How do operating systems in edge devices facilitate real-time processing and low-latency responses to data?

Answer: Operating systems in edge devices are often designed to prioritize real-time and low-latency processing. They manage resources efficiently, minimize background tasks, and support real-time scheduling.

4. What are the key benefits of edge computing in terms of data privacy, security, and bandwidth efficiency?

Answer: Edge computing enhances data privacy and security by processing sensitive data locally. It reduces the need to transmit large amounts of data to the cloud, conserving bandwidth.

5. Explain the term "fog computing" and its relationship with edge computing.

Answer: Fog computing is an extension of edge computing that includes a hierarchical approach to processing data at multiple layers of the network, combining local edge devices and nearby fog nodes for computing tasks.

6. What are some use cases for edge computing, and how do they benefit from local data processing?

Answer: Use cases include autonomous vehicles, industrial automation, smart cities, and remote monitoring. They benefit from edge computing by reducing response times and enabling real-time decision-making.

7. How do operating systems on edge devices handle resource constraints and optimize system performance in resource-limited environments?

Answer: Edge OSs optimize performance by efficiently managing resources, supporting low-power modes, and implementing minimalistic code to operate effectively in resource-constrained environments.

8. What is the role of edge gateways in edge computing, and how do they interact with edge device operating systems?

Answer: Edge gateways act as intermediaries between edge devices and the central cloud. They aggregate data, provide local processing, and communicate with the cloud. Edge device operating systems work in tandem with edge gateways to ensure efficient data flow.

9. What are some challenges in managing and securing edge devices and operating systems in distributed edge computing environments?

Answer: Challenges include device heterogeneity, security concerns, remote updates, and device monitoring. Edge device OSs must be designed to address these challenges effectively.

10. Explain the importance of software-defined networking (SDN) and virtualization in edge computing environments and their role in managing edge device operating systems.

Answer: SDN and virtualization enable flexible network management and the dynamic allocation of resources in edge computing. They assist in managing and scaling edge device operating systems to meet the demands of varying workloads.

Serverless Computing

1. What is serverless computing, and how does it differ from traditional server-based computing?

Answer: Serverless computing is a cloud computing model where cloud providers manage infrastructure, automatically scaling and managing resources based on application demand. It differs from traditional server-based computing where developers are responsible for provisioning and managing servers.

2. Explain the concept of a "function" in serverless computing and how it fits into the serverless model.

Answer: A function in serverless computing is a small, self-contained piece of code that performs a specific task. Functions are the building blocks of serverless applications, and they are executed in response to events, without the need to manage servers.

3. What is an event trigger, and how do serverless platforms use triggers to execute functions?

Answer: An event trigger is a specific occurrence that initiates the execution of a function. Serverless platforms use triggers to respond to various events, such as HTTP requests, database changes, or file uploads, by invoking the corresponding function.

4. How does serverless computing help organizations optimize costs and resource utilization compared to traditional server-based hosting?

Answer: Serverless computing reduces costs by automatically allocating and de-allocating resources based on usage. This eliminates the need for continuously running and maintaining servers, making it a cost-effective model.

5. Explain the concept of auto-scaling in serverless computing and how it ensures performance under varying workloads.

Answer: Auto-scaling in serverless computing automatically adjusts the number of function instances based on the incoming workload. This ensures consistent performance and responsiveness without manual intervention.

6. What are some popular serverless computing platforms, and how do they differ in terms of features and integrations?

Answer: Popular serverless platforms include AWS Lambda, Azure Functions, Google Cloud Functions, and others. They differ in terms of supported programming languages, integrations with other cloud services, and available triggers.

7. How do serverless operating systems manage the deployment and execution of functions in a serverless environment?

Answer: Serverless operating systems, often provided by cloud providers, manage function deployment, execution, and resource allocation. They handle the orchestration of functions in response to triggers.

8. What are the advantages and limitations of serverless computing for different types of applications and workloads?

Answer: Serverless computing is advantageous for applications with varying workloads and sporadic usage, but it may not be ideal for long-running or resource-intensive tasks due to resource constraints and cold start times.

9. Explain the concept of "cold start" in serverless computing and how it can impact application performance.

Answer: A cold start occurs when a serverless function is invoked for the first time or after an idle period. It can impact performance as the function needs to initialize, causing a slight delay.

10. What are some security considerations in serverless computing, and how do organizations address these concerns?

Answer: Security considerations include function isolation, access controls, and secure handling of data. Organizations address these concerns by implementing proper access policies, encryption, and security best practices specific to their serverless environment

Quantum Computing and OS Challenges

1. What is quantum computing, and how does it differ from classical computing?

Answer: Quantum computing leverages the principles of quantum mechanics to perform computations using quantum bits (qubits) instead of classical bits. Unlike classical computers, quantum computers can process information in superposition and entanglement states, potentially solving certain problems much faster.

2. What are some of the key challenges in integrating quantum computing with traditional operating systems?

Answer: Challenges include:

Coordinating the interaction between classical and quantum processing units.

Handling qubit errors and ensuring fault tolerance.

Adapting classical algorithms to leverage quantum processing.

3. How does quantum computing impact the security and encryption protocols used by traditional operating systems?

Answer: Quantum computers have the potential to break existing encryption schemes, leading to increased emphasis on post-quantum cryptography and the need to develop new secure protocols.

4. Explain the concept of quantum supremacy and its implications for operating systems.

Answer: Quantum supremacy is the milestone where quantum computers can solve problems faster than classical computers. It has implications for traditional operating systems, as they need to support quantum hardware and interact with it efficiently.

5. What is the role of error correction in quantum computing, and how does it affect the operating system's interaction with quantum hardware?

Answer: Error correction is crucial in quantum computing to mitigate the impact of qubit errors. The operating system must coordinate error correction processes and ensure that quantum computations remain reliable.

6. How does quantum computing impact the execution of specific algorithms and tasks within traditional operating systems?

Answer: Certain algorithms, such as those related to cryptography and optimization, may benefit significantly from quantum computing. The operating system must provide the infrastructure to execute these quantum-enhanced algorithms.

7. What are the resource requirements for quantum computing, and how does an operating system manage these resources efficiently?

Answer: Quantum computing requires specialized hardware and low-temperature environments. The operating system must allocate resources, handle job queues, and ensure efficient resource utilization.

8. What are the programming languages and tools used in quantum computing, and how does the operating system facilitate their integration?

Answer: Quantum programming languages like Qiskit and Cirq are used in quantum computing. The operating system must provide support for these languages, as well as integration with quantum development kits and simulators.

9. Explain the concept of quantum virtual machines and how they can be integrated into traditional operating systems.

Answer: Quantum virtual machines are software tools that simulate quantum computation. Integrating them into traditional operating systems enables testing and development of quantum algorithms in controlled environments.

10. What are some potential applications of quantum computing in traditional operating systems, and how can they impact various industries?

Answer: Potential applications include cryptography, optimization, drug discovery, and material science. Quantum computing can revolutionize these industries by solving complex problems faster and more efficiently. Operating systems play a key role in enabling these applications.

ONLINE RESOURCES

Practice Paper Link: https://forms.gle/2iDkNpvuZkCxJRSY7

QR Code:

VideoLink: https://www.youtube.com/playlist?list=PLzlh_31VWEFrbG7j2P110p6mHDCHaXECO

QR Code:

Chapter 11: Types of Operating Systems

Linux

1. What is Linux, and how does it differ from other operating systems?

Answer: Linux is an open-source operating system kernel that serves as the foundation for various Linux distributions. It differs from other operating systems in its open-source nature, flexibility, and wide range of distributions tailored for specific use cases.

2. Explain the difference between the Linux kernel and a Linux distribution.

Answer: The Linux kernel is the core part of the operating system that manages hardware resources. A Linux distribution, often called a distro, includes the kernel, system utilities, libraries, and applications, packaged together to form a complete operating system.

3. What is the command-line interface (CLI) in Linux, and how does it differ from the graphical user interface (GUI)?

Answer: The CLI is a text-based interface for interacting with the operating system, where commands are entered in a terminal. The GUI is a graphical interface with windows, icons, and buttons. Linux provides both CLI and GUI options, with the CLI being more powerful for system administration.

4. Explain the concept of open source in Linux and its significance.

Answer: Open source means that the source code of Linux is freely available, allowing anyone to view, modify, and distribute it. This fosters collaboration, innovation, and a strong community of developers, making Linux highly customizable and secure.

5. What are the major components of a Linux file system, and how is it organized?

Answer: The major components include directories, files, and links. The Linux file system is organized hierarchically, starting from the root directory (/) and branching into subdirectories.

6. What is the role of package managers in Linux, and can you name a few popular package managers and the distributions they are associated with?

Answer: Package managers are tools for installing, updating, and managing software packages. Popular package managers include APT (Debian/Ubuntu), YUM/DNF (Fedora), and Pacman (Arch Linux).

7. Explain the permissions system in Linux file systems, including the use of permission bits and file ownership.

Answer: Linux file permissions consist of three sets of permission bits (read, write, execute) for the owner, group, and others. Ownership is determined by the user and group associated with a file, enabling fine-grained control over access.

8. What is the role of a shell in Linux, and how does it facilitate interaction with the operating system?

Answer: A shell is a command-line interpreter that allows users to interact with the Linux OS by executing commands and scripts. Popular Linux shells include Bash, Zsh, and Fish.

9. What is a Linux runlevel, and how does it relate to system booting and initialization?

Answer: Runlevels are states in which a Linux system can operate. They define which services and daemons are started during the system boot process. Runlevel 3, for instance, is often used for multi-user mode without a GUI.

10. Explain the role of the /etc/passwd and /etc/shadow files in user management in Linux.

Answer: The /etc/passwd file stores user account information, while the /etc/shadow file stores password hashes and other security-related data. Together, they manage user authentication and access control in Linux.

Unix

1. What is Unix, and how does it differ from other operating systems?

Answer: Unix is a family of operating systems known for its multitasking and multiuser capabilities. It differs from other operating systems in its design philosophy of small, modular tools that can be combined to perform complex tasks.

2. Explain the concept of the Unix shell and its role in interacting with the operating system.

Answer: The Unix shell is a command-line interface that allows users to interact with the Unix operating system. It interprets user commands and provides access to system resources and utilities.

3. What is the Unix file hierarchy, and how is it organized?

Answer: Unix organizes its file system hierarchy starting from the root directory (/) and branching into subdirectories. Key directories include /bin (binary executables), /home (user directories), and /etc (system configuration files).

4. What are some of the key features of Unix-like operating systems, and how do they contribute to its popularity?

Answer: Key features include multitasking, multiuser support, a powerful command-line interface, modular design, and a large library of available tools. These features make Unix-like systems versatile and adaptable.

5. Explain the permissions system in Unix file systems, including the use of permission bits and file ownership.

Answer: Unix file permissions consist of three sets of permission bits (read, write, execute) for the owner, group, and others. Ownership is determined by the user and group associated with a file, allowing fine-grained access control.

6. What is a Unix process, and how does the operating system manage and control processes?

Answer: A Unix process is a running instance of a program. The operating system manages and controls processes through system calls, scheduling, and process management tools.

7. What is the role of a Unix shell script, and how does it differ from a regular program?

Answer: A Unix shell script is a series of Unix commands saved in a file. It is executed by a shell and provides automation of tasks. Unlike regular programs, shell scripts are interpreted and do not require compilation.

8. Explain the concept of Unix pipes, and how do they enable data communication between commands?

Answer: Unix pipes allow the output of one command to be used as the input for another. They facilitate the seamless flow of data between multiple commands, enabling complex data processing.

9. What is the purpose of the /etc/passwd and /etc/shadow files in Unix-based systems, and how do they manage user accounts and passwords?

Answer: The /etc/passwd file stores user account information, while the /etc/shadow file stores password hashes and security-related data. Together, they manage user authentication and access control in Unix-based systems.

10. Explain the concept of a Unix shell prompt and some common Unix shells used in the operating system.

Answer: A Unix shell prompt is the text or symbol that appears to indicate that the shell is ready to accept commands. Common Unix shells include the Bourne shell (sh), the Bourne-Again shell (bash), the C shell (csh), and the Korn shell (ksh). Each has its own features and syntax.

Shell

1. What is a shell in the context of operating systems, and what is its primary function?

Answer: A shell is a command-line interface that provides a user-friendly way to interact with an operating system. Its primary function is to interpret and execute commands and scripts entered by the user.

2. Explain the difference between a shell and an operating system.

Answer: An operating system is the core software that manages computer hardware and provides a foundation for all software. A shell is an interface that runs on top of the operating system, allowing users to interact with it and run commands.

3. What are the key characteristics of a shell script, and how does it differ from a compiled program?

Answer: Shell scripts are text files containing a series of shell commands. They are interpreted at runtime, rather than compiled, making them more human-readable and versatile.

4. Name some popular Unix/Linux shells and describe their unique features.

Answer: Popular shells include:

Bash (Bourne-Again Shell): Known for its widespread use and scripting capabilities.

Zsh (Z Shell): Offers advanced customization and features like autocompletion.

Fish (Friendly Interactive Shell): Designed for a user-friendly experience with intuitive syntax.

5. Explain the concept of shell scripting, and provide an example of a task that can be automated with a shell script.

Answer: Shell scripting is the practice of writing scripts that execute a series of shell commands. An example task is automating system backups, where a script can compress and archive files, then store them at specified locations.

6. What is a shebang (#!) line in a shell script, and why is it important?

Answer: The shebang line is the first line of a script and specifies the interpreter to use. For example, #!/bin/bash indicates that the script should be interpreted using the Bash shell. It's crucial for ensuring the correct interpreter is used.

7. How do variables work in shell scripts, and what are their scopes and naming conventions?

Answer: Variables in shell scripts are used to store and manipulate data. They have global or local scope, depending on how they are declared. Variable names are typically written in uppercase letters by convention.

8. Explain the use of control structures in shell scripts, including loops and conditional statements.

Answer: Control structures like for and while loops and if and case conditional statements are used to control the flow of a script. They enable decision-making and repetitive tasks.

9. What is the purpose of input/output redirection in shell scripts, and how can it be used to manipulate data streams?

Answer: Input/output redirection allows the script to send output to files or receive input from files, making it a powerful tool for processing and manipulating data streams.

10. What are functions in shell scripts, and how do they aid in code organization and reusability?

Answer: Functions are named blocks of code within a script that can be called multiple times. They aid in code organization and reusability by encapsulating specific tasks or operations.

Windows

1. What do you consider your greatest strengths?

Answer: One of my greatest strengths is my ability to problem-solve effectively. I enjoy tackling complex challenges and finding innovative solutions. Additionally, I'm a strong communicator, which helps me collaborate well with team members and clients.

2. What's your approach to handling tight deadlines and high-pressure situations?

Answer: When facing tight deadlines or high-pressure situations, I prioritize tasks and break them into manageable steps. I communicate with the team to ensure everyone is on the same page and work efficiently to meet the deadline. It's also important to remain calm and focused under pressure.

3. Can you describe a project or accomplishment that you're particularly proud of?

Answer: One project I'm proud of is when I led a team to develop a mobile app for a client with a tight timeline. We successfully delivered the project ahead of schedule and received positive feedback from the client. It demonstrated our team's commitment and ability to deliver under pressure.

4. What programming languages and technologies are you most proficient in?

Answer: I'm proficient in JavaScript, Python, and SQL. I have extensive experience with front-end frameworks like React and Angular, and I'm skilled in using databases like PostgreSQL and MongoDB.

5. How do you stay updated on industry trends and emerging technologies?

Answer: I stay updated by regularly reading tech blogs, following industry news, and participating in online communities and forums. I also take online courses and attend conferences to learn about new technologies and best practices.

6. Tell me about a time when you had to work in a diverse team. How did you handle it?

Answer: In a previous role, I collaborated with team members from diverse cultural backgrounds. I ensured effective communication by being respectful, listening actively, and valuing different perspectives. It enriched our problem-solving and creativity.

7. What's your approach to debugging and troubleshooting when encountering a complex issue in your code?

Answer: When facing a complex issue, I start by reviewing the code and logs to identify the root cause. I break down the problem into smaller parts and test each component to isolate the issue. I also consult with colleagues or online communities for fresh insights.

8. How do you prioritize tasks when working on multiple projects simultaneously?

Answer: I use project management tools to create task lists and prioritize based on deadlines, importance, and dependencies. Regular communication with project stakeholders helps me stay aligned with project goals and adjust priorities as needed.

9. Where do you see your career in the next 5 years?

Answer: In the next five years, I see myself taking on more leadership roles, potentially as a team lead or project manager. I'm also interested in continuing my education and staying updated on emerging technologies to remain at the forefront of my field.

ONLINE RESOURCES

Practice Paper Link: **https://forms.gle/kn3jZftYQCacmTov6**

QR Code:

Video Link: **https://www.youtube.com/playlist?list=PLzlh_31VWEFqmjq7PBRbdX4bens_lgnbO**

QR Code:

YouTube Videos Playlists for all Chapters

1. CHAPTER 1

Link : https://www.youtube.com/playlist?list=PLzlh_31VWEFqv1VgO4t3ClJJUIWrFeGU7

QR Code:

2. CHAPTER 2

Link: https://www.youtube.com/playlist?list=PLzlh_31VWEFqxHZkYsZ6Xy_dFG4IHwBDg

QR Code:

3. CHAPTER 3

Link: https://www.youtube.com/playlist?list=PLzlh_31VWEFpIj9tSbhkG9PHg2ZEG26NQ .

QR Code:

4. CHAPTER 4

Link:https://www.youtube.com/playlist?list=PLzlh_31VWEFr0nhNKvQouAwg1OdvsTSMu

QR Code:

5. CHAPTER 5

Link : https://www.youtube.com/playlist?list=PLzlh_31VWEFpYotpexo0YDwU1qUtbFYUv

QR Code:

6. CHAPTER 6

Link : https://www.youtube.com/playlist?list=PLzlh_31VWEFq2JYMcMOyDkMIOGQabt8_8

QR Code:

7. CHAPTER 7

Link: https://www.youtube.com/playlist?list=PLzlh_31VWEFq-auuAtOHhZfCMKEeKtrb8

QR Code:

8. CHAPTER 8

Link: https://www.youtube.com/playlist?list=PLzlh_31VWEFpVk0I2Ux9gausDx0oTYDru .

QR Code:

9. CHAPTER 9

Link: https://www.youtube.com/playlist?list=PLzlh_31VWEFof7DpbLyhvLatMoborYWz8 .

QR Code:

10. CHAPTER 10

Link: https://www.youtube.com/playlist?list=PLzlh_31VWEFrbG7j2P110p6mHDCHaXECO

QR Code:

11. CHAPTER 11

Link : **https://www.youtube.com/playlist?list=PLzlh_31VWEFqmIRaa058F7muPVIKLSUoV**

QR Code:

Operating System Interview Questions & Answers Playlist:
Link:https://www.youtube.com/playlist?list=PLzlh_31VWEFrnzlxBBmM5RY_c42ltriCE

QR Code:

Operating System Playlist:

Link: https://www.youtube.com/playlist?list=PLzlh_31VWEFoZUJQ_f2U6gaug4W_KGRm1

QR Code: